THANK GOD I HAVE A TEENAGER

THANK GOD I HAVE A TEENAGER

Charles S. Mueller

AUGSBURG Publishing House • Minneapolis

THANK GOD I HAVE A TEENAGER

Scripture quotations unless otherwise noted are from The Good News Bible, Today's English Version, copyright 1966, 1971, 1976 by the American Bible Society. Used by permission.

Library of Congress Cataloging in Publication Data

Mueller, Charles S.
  THANK GOD I HAVE A TEENAGER.

  1. Youth—United States—Social conditions.
2. Parenting—United States. 3. Family—United
States—Religious life. I. Title.
HQ796.M8325 1985   305.2'35   84-24363
ISBN 0-8066-2126-5 (Pbk.)

Manufactured in the U.S.A.   APH 10-6239

        3   4   5   6   7   8   9   0   1   2   3   4   5   6   7   8   9

To Audrey,
the one who walked with me and
taught me so much as we, together,
learned how great teenagers really are.

Contents

Preface

I'm convinced that most adults, many parents included, are afraid of teenagers.

There could be a dozen reasons for their feelings. Do they remember their own youths and in the memories find cause for fear? Have they had sad experiences with a teenager or heard of someone who has? Are they nervously anticipating the changed relationship that the coming teen years of their kids will bring to their families?

I want to help any interested adult, especially a mom or dad, get past all negative feelings toward teenagers and the teen years. I want to help them say, with informed and genuine conviction, "Thank God I have a teenager to share and grow with."

Sound farfetched? Impossible? Stick with me. You can learn to say that—with joy.

It might help you accept my assistance if I tell you a little about myself and the background from which I write.

I am married. My wife and I have had the pleasure of rearing four children to adulthood. Three are already out of their teens and married. A fourth will soon join them in both conditions.

I'm a pastor. I've always worked with young people and liked them. I've never been a youth "specialist." Purely by accident—and then only when I was well into my 40s—I became seriously involved in a large-scale ministry to young people. I started speaking before large groups of teens. (By large groups I mean 500, 1000, 3000.) For the last 10 or 15 years I've been caught up in a coast-to-coast, border-to-border ministry that has taken me to almost every major city at least once and dropped me into the world of teens month in and month out.

I've talked and I've written. Teens have listened and read. In doing both they have blessed me by their attentiveness and exhilarating response. Their response in attendance (I call that voting with your feet), their attentiveness (the place is quiet but they are not asleep), their embarrassingly vigorous applause (they sure know how to let you know they like something), and their many notes, letters, sharings, conversations, questions, and comments have all assured me I've been on target.

I've also listened. I've watched. I've studied. After listening, watching, and studying, I've tried to do whatever seemed appropriate. One of the best ministries I have been able to offer my thousands of young friends is a ready ear—and reserved judgment. Young people don't meet very many adults who actually listen and who hold back swift decisions of right or wrong.

I've learned from my teen friends and also from men like Dr. Ray Bardill, with whom I wrote *Thank God I'm a Teenager* (Augsburg, 1976). He especially helped me see and understand the terrifyingly low self-image many young people have. It shouldn't be surprising. Whoever tells a kid he or she is great? And loved? And trusted?

I've also learned from those who do specialize—from youth workers. These heroes and heroines are usually young, conspicuously Christian, excitingly creative, and incredibly caring. They are also fun. They do more relation building with laughter and games and songs than I think a thousand preachers accomplish with as many sermons. In the process of having fun, these tremendous youth workers help develop the kind of young Christian men and women that teenagers actually *are*.

I've learned from our national leaders of youth. Most of them are my age. All of them have hearts and spirits that are young and a great tenderness for young people. To mention some is to leave out many, but I must say at least a few names aloud: Larry Johnson, Rich Bimler, Leo Symmank, Cliff Pedersen, Dave Anderson, Dean Damman, Aron Vallesky, Ben Eggers, Bill Ameiss, Ed Birner, and many others. Right behind them in terms of age (but they're equal in every other way) are dozens of other well-trained regional youth leaders from every part of the United States. And pressing forward from behind them are hundreds of other helpers of teenagers—who want to help parents too.

Now let's get down to specifics. In this book I've tried to lay out the most helpful parental materials I know. In doing so I have sought a sequential approach, but that's not fully possible. In dealing with teens, there are so many "beginnings" of understanding. We have to start in a number of places almost simultaneously. Chapter 1 makes an early and critical point: things are not the way they used to be. The world has changed—in many ways. People who deny that believe that no one quite understands what's happening but themselves—and that's very lonely.

Chapter 2 has a parallel assertion: all parents, individually, have changed too. They have been changing all along and will keep changing the rest of their lives. I still am amazed how many adults think that after 21 the only thing that really changes with them is that they get wrinkles! Wrinkles are almost the least of the changes that all adults experience and that, if not understood, can be very confusing and destructive.

When you've handled those two chapters, you're ready to deal more specifically with teens. Chapters 3 and 4 are a one-two punch: teens as they aren't, and teens as they are.

We spend so much time reacting to myths about teenagers that we generally miss the chances to enjoy and understand the reality of the teen years. Those two chapters will help correct difficulties in those directions.

Chapters 5 through 8 are about teen parenting in specific and family life in general. They develop *(a)* what Scripture teaches us about teens, using the example of the world's greatest teenager—Jesus Christ; *(b)* basic skills that help healing in slightly banged-up families (and keep families from hurting themselves further as well); *(c)* encouragement to listen as Christ tells all of us to " . . . love your neighbor as yourself"; and finally *(d)* three crucial insights that make life with your teenager livable.

So there you have it. I hope you'll walk with me all the way. It won't be toward an end; it will be toward a beginning. Beyond the last page are so many new things in your life that you will wonder how you got along without them. All of these new things will improve and bless you, and the teenagers around you, for years to come.

My goal? It's simple. I want to help every Christian parent say (or say again), "Thank God I have a teenager."

My special thanks to Nelda Piper and Judy White for the caring ministry of typing and typing and typing. Their skilled work and helpful insights have blessed me and will surely bless you.

Enough of an introduction. Let's be on with the task in the name of the triune God: Father, Son, and Holy Spirit. To God be the glory.

1 It Ain't Like It Used to Be

Excuse my grammar. This chapter title comes from a story of a Tulsa, Oklahoma, pastor, Harold Brockhoff. An old farmer from the panhandle of that state was asked how things were going. He paused a moment and summarized his analysis in three sentences: "Well, it ain't like it used to be. And it ain't like it ought to be. But it ain't like it's gonna be either!"

It ain't. We've changed. Change is a fact. It is a continuing, irrefutable fact. Refuse to face change and you have refused to face life.

I'm not saying anything new. Heraclitus, a philosopher who taught in Greece years before Christ was born, stated the principle of continuous change in two words, "Everything flows." He contended that you can't step into the same river twice. By the time you step in and step out and then step in again, the river has flowed on. It's a different river. And you are not the same person you were even a second or so before.

If, instead of envisioning a person stepping in and out of a river, you think of someone trying to step back into one of life's past experiences, you can quickly recognize that the philosopher's words are true. People aren't the same as they were when they were young. The streets of today aren't the same. The news isn't the same. The choices aren't the same. Nothing is identical to the way it was. Everything has changed—is changing—will change.

Don't think of those last paragraphs as some kind of abstract philosophical meandering that you can take or leave depending on your mood of the moment. That would be dangerous. Misunderstanding the message of Heraclitus or refusing to accept the truth of the Oklahoma farmer's synopsis of life is a guarantee of misunderstanding most things that happen in life, whether today, tomorrow, or a thousand years ago.

Those who want to mope about, clucking about how bad things have become since they were 16, can do so. Much of that mood is a result of idealizing the past. Their distorted perspective of *then* twists their understanding of *now*. Living with flawed memories, they sacrifice most of their potential usefulness in helping today's young people. Whatever else we can say about today's teens, one thing is absolute and certain: they are *today's* teens. If we are to assist them, and if they are going to help us, they must be understood in this historical moment's reality—a world considerably changed since we older ones walked in their chronological shoes.

Let me put it another way. Life is not a snapshot; it's a moving picture. Life is dynamic. It has motion. Hard on the heels of our yesterday is a brand-new and different today, with an even more varied tomorrow waiting in the wings. In each dawn, life's realities shift ever so slightly, and much of what we are must be realigned. Life changes. People change. Though it would seem obvious, it still needs to be stated: you change.

Want to argue about all that? You can if you wish. You can deny it too. You can state that the moral, legal, social, and educational expectations of your own teenage years are the same as those of today. But if that is your position, you're out of the teenage discussion, and you're on your own, alone. You don't want that.

OK! I accept reality. What shall I do? Complain? Disagree? Debate whether the situation now is better or worse? For the moment let's do none of these things. Instead let's just inspect change. Let's look at it—closely. Let's see what can be learned. To help this happen, I'll list the things that my contact with young people and my experience as a pastor dealing with families would suggest are very important areas of fundamental change. They look so harmless that they are often overlooked.

Fundamental change one: clothing and hairstyles

Clothing and hairstyles are different from when you were young. Absolutely! These two things constantly change. They always have. This is the easiest area in which succeeding waves of young people quickly create new and special identities. A trip to the barber. A change of clothes. A "new" person. Instant results.

Clothing and hairstyles have been the battleground of parental/teenage tension since Roman days. Parents complained about their children's tonsorial and sartorial aberrations in Latin! Right now things are rather quiet, but 10 or 12 years ago you could get an instant fight by bringing up long hair (or short) and kids' crazy clothing. But why? Why do people especially argue about those two things? And why has it been going on for so long?

Most arguments about those things are not a question of right or wrong, though parents and kids like to make them so. The fighting is actually tied to *assertiveness* and/or *dominance*. From the youngster's point of view, it's a matter of assertiveness ("I want to be me!"). From the parental point of view it's a matter of concerned dominance (". . . because I'm your father, that's why!").

The best way to keep your parental cool about hairstyles and clothes is to learn a lesson from the past. If the fight is old, maybe some of the insight can be just as old. There's an old Latin saying: "There's no point arguing about taste." I'm guessing that expression was first spit out by a disgusted Roman parent after a heated subject on long hair and short togas.

If you think things are out of kilter today, page through some older books and newspapers. Look in the library! Or look through your family photo album—at you! Seek out a Sears or Wards catalog of the '50s or earlier. Review the evidence. Each one of these items is a repository of what good and godly folk used to wear and how they styled their hair. Don't they look absurd today? Let those pages and pictures remind you that standards shift. They always have.

If there must be a debate about hair and clothing, then argue whether families yesterday used to argue more about bobby sox than families today do about blue jeans; whether there was more tension about crew cuts on the baseball team then than about a pony-tailed quarterback now. And mark this in your book of useful insight: any family squabble about clothing and hairstyle is not only centuries old, *but it is a quagmire from which no one emerges the victor.* Those two subjects make for splendid family sharing, for funny family conversation. But as an area of serious family squabbling, they make for deadly and destructive confrontation. Stay away. Comfort yourself with the sure knowledge that—you guessed it!—things will change.

Fundamental change two: music

Don't argue with your kids about music either. I agree with you that today's music is loud and seems generally incomprehensible. But it's also a significant place for staking out teenage identity. Comfort yourself with the knowledge that most teenagers, once they become full-fledged adults, improve their musical tastes and find other ways to express their inner feelings. And comfort yourself right now with the confidence that you already know of other, and better, music. Once the teen years pass, each generation seems to accept the better expression of time's musical forms.

For now feel free to go ahead and turn down the volume (it hurts my ears too) and mumble to yourself, "I wish they still had the same great music there used to be on the radio when I was a teenager." In the mumbling you have become one with your own father and mother who undoubtedly had the same feelings about your musical tastes some years ago.

But you may also take a more positive approach. Why not become better acquainted with the music that now appeals to your son or daughter? While interviewing teenagers on TV a number of years ago, I discovered that music was one of the few subjects most teenagers could discuss at length. That's understandable. They are still developing knowledge. Adults usually exhaust teenagers' conversational capabilities in most other areas rather quickly, but kids can speak at length about music. If you have trouble communicating with your teenager, it will pay you to become acquainted with their music—and use it as a basis for conversation.

One last thing. As you actually listen to their music, you have an excellent chance to talk with them about its message. Sometimes it is terrible. But they usually don't "hear" the words. Now, if *you* listen carefully, you have a great chance to discuss with them the Christian perspective of the song's theme. But it's on their turf then, not yours. That makes talking easier.

Fundamental change three: marriage, family, and the American home

Are you surprised when I tell you that marriage, family, and the American home are experiencing significant change? Studies are surfacing that puncture many previously popular preconceptions about good homes. For instance, do you believe there is a relationship between unhappiness of children and mothers who work? Early studies suggest that's not true. Do you believe that it's better for children that parents divorce rather than stay married and expose them to a semiunhappy condition? The message of many studies seems to say, "Stay married while you do something about your problem." Do you believe that it's better to live together before the marriage ceremony to test out your potential compatibility as a husband or wife? A fascinating result of studies on that topic is that there are slightly more divorces among those who have lived together before marriage than those who have not. These and many other myths about home, family, and marriage need confrontation and open discussion.

The skyrocketing divorce rates also have a major impact on teenagers. Last summer I spoke before a large youth gathering in Colorado. In one of the optional sectional presentations to some of the 1,200 teenagers gathered, I was asked to share about communicating with parents. I was surprised how many attended. During the presentation, on instinct, I asked, "How many of you are living in a single-parent family?" Hands shot up all over the auditorium. Nearly all came from *single-parent homes!*

There in the Rockies, on neutral ground with no parents in attendance, these young men and women poured out their hearts. I learned a lot about marriage, family, and homes from some who had seen them fail—firsthand. It was obvious these young men and women had not come through the termination of their parents' marriages unscathed. Some were angry. Many felt personal responsibility for the divorces and would prove, with all kinds of interesting and convoluted reasoning, that they were the causes. A few were struggling with the problem of choosing between parents. Kids thought there was a lot of bad advice in the world coming from the "specialists" who approved actions that they, as immediate participants, knew were wrong. It was a hurt, confused, and angry crowd.

Most will survive. I hope all will forgive. I don't believe any will forget.

The single-parent family is not new, but today's reason for the single-parent family is. A hundred years ago death was the family destroyer. Now it's divorce. Homes are "voluntarily" destroyed! That's new. And the destruction is at a previously unheard-of rate. That's new. Together those facts spell C-H-A-N-G-E.

Fundamental change four: fewer parental models

All of us learn from example. It's as simple as that. When you want to determine what to do in any given situation, the first thing you reflect upon is how your parents did it. Then, using their example as the style for a right or wrong approach, you move ahead.

Fundamental Change Four is related to the previous section: thousands of young people are growing up in a world where they have no present parental model to fall back on. Their mothers or their fathers are simply not in the house. They have no observable models. As a specific application of this, and as advice to parents, if your son or daughter marries someone who comes from a divorced home, be ready to help when they face situations for which their memory has no model! Memory makes for models, and models make for an easier life.

The problem of this change can be illustrated like this: suppose you gave a person a book of instructions for successful living and then tore out random pages. Maybe he or she could piece together what's missing and maybe not. The best hope would be finding someone who could fill in the missing pages. This paste-and-patch approach will work, but it's not the same as the real thing.

The absence of one parental model or the other in many homes is the reason why I now spend so much of my pastoral time in premarital preparations. I can almost assume that one of the two who are to be married will be from a single-parent family. Working from the belief that the best way to keep a marriage together is by making sure it doesn't come apart, the couple and I try to identify as many supportive models for their marriage as we can. That's tough work. But you can help people like me help your children when they marry. How? Through your marriage.

Your marriage is a powerful teaching tool (whether you intend it to be or not!) for your teenage son or daughter. Talk with your marriage partner about whether your marriage is a solid and sound commitment (and thus a good model) or whether it's creaking in some or all of its parts. If your marriage is coming apart, the teenagers ought to be given access to the problems and the decision-making process. They need to have a clean shot at helping you make your marriage work, because it absolutely affects them.

If the marriage is over and you are now divorced, talk with them about that too. Don't spend time berating your former spouse. Tell your children the truth about what happened as dispassionately as you are able. You can at least be the model of an honest, concerned, divorced parent.

Fundamental change five: nuclear war

Nuclear war? Teenagers? Ridiculous! I first picked up on this change in mental perception among teenagers while speaking before 700 teens on Mackinac Island, Michigan, during the summer of 1981. It was the summer before nuclear concern really started surfacing. The place we met was Michigan, a heartland state. I always ask kids to write me notes about what concerns them. It was at this gathering that a series of notes first popped up about an atomic holocaust.

My initial reaction, shared by other adults present, was that somehow or another a recent movie or TV program had stirred their concern. We checked that out and found it was not so. A few months later, that same sensitivity began surfacing all over the United States. It's worldwide now. People conducting opinion polls and surveys are finding similar feelings everywhere. Whatever your personal attitude in the matter, there is a genuine voiced concern by the nation's youth about nuclear war. They expect it. They dread it.

Assume my observations are correct. Can you imagine how this will affect a young person's decisions? At the very least, I suspect dread of nuclear war has been a contributing factor to the unusually high number of young men who have declined to register for the draft. Hundreds of thousands have made that choice. I also sense a hesitation among young people about long-range planning and discussions of the far future. Goals for life, decisions about family-to-be, choices for jobs—all are increasingly colored by nuclear war's brooding shadow.

Having made those unsettling observations about nuclear war, I don't want to walk away without suggesting some things that parents can do. First of all, *let the concern surface.* Don't quash the subject. Talk about it. There is no advantage to brushing war or nuclear war aside. All that will happen then is that your son or daughter won't discuss their fears anymore—with you. What could make for better communication than showing your son or daughter that you, too, are struggling with the same concern?

If you can't talk about it, for whatever reason, be sure that you make that point. Say simply, "I just can't talk about that." Give the reason if you can. That's much better than sidestepping the concern.

Another suggestion for a family project is to review the lessons of history. Read a book together, like Barbara Tuchman's *The Distant Mirror* or *The Guns of August,* or something by Bruce Catton on the Civil War. History shows us that people have always been dogged by brutal problems, most of their own making. Since those first mistakes in the Garden of Eden, there have been deadly difficulties, whether the immediate enemy was Cain, or Sennacharib, or Caiphas, or Caesar Augustus. The Bible is also the story of people who walked in danger all the way. The intense beauty of many psalms is shaped by the promise God offers to people under the most difficult conditions. A family study of Psalm 46 or Psalm 130 could be marvelous.

Before you let the subject of nuclear war get away from you, consider the potential it has as an excellent and uniting arena for family sharing. Use this change to your advantage.

Fundamental change six: college, or what?

Not too many years ago there were no real educational choices. Things were quite uncomplicated. You either *(a)* went to college and got a job or *(b)* did not go to college and got a job.

Now that decision is more complicated. Kids are asking whether college is worth it at all. Will it make any difference? Some write, "If I go to college, will I have a job when I graduate?" They worry about what will happen if they choose the wrong field and, after spending $20,000 or more, discover they have majored in a field whose potential has narrowed considerably during their college days.

Other young people wonder whether, if they skip a college education and go immediately into the work force, their jobs will last long enough to complete full careers. For fun, make a list of the number of vocations you can guarantee will be around when your son or daughter is considering retirement in the 21st century. Not many! There is a swelling number of adults who, after years of service to one company or in one vocation, are discovering that their employers are closing the plants or that their particular skills are no longer required. Many of the unemployed who are presently furloughed will never be recalled to their former tasks. *Their* jobs are gone.

It's been a long time since we have had serious debates on the value of college education. Over most of my ministerial career it's been assumed that there was considerable financial advantage to higher education. Whether that was true or not then, a lot of people are questioning whether it's true now. Moving into a period of increased educational costs, increased job instability, increased vocational and career choices that require specific kinds of decisions, young people are struggling.

Help your young person think through the vocational/educational questions of our time. Don't just turn them over to some kind of an advisor. Who knows your youngster better than you? Together see what you can learn about what the future holds in terms of vocation. Take advantage of this change too.

More change

This could be the longest chapter in any book ever written. Change is everywhere. One change that deserves considerable attention, and which is best dealt with at home, is women's rights. Think of the changes in women's rights in just the last few years, and the changes that must yet be made. They will affect home, family, women, men, children, parents—everybody. Yet change doesn't seem to happen in this field as quickly and radically as those who care would like. Parents need to help daughters recognize and understand what they face.

We're getting older as a nation—that's a change. The average age of the United States population is on the rise. There is an increasing number of older folks around. This could be a splendid moment for discovering one of the greatest family reinforcements in all history: the presence of the elderly.

A lot of elderly are coming down the road! One of the most electric sentences I've heard in the last few years is: "If you're 50, you're going to be 90." Think of that. That means we'll be around a long time. Young people preparing for marriage should seriously contemplate celebrating their 75th wedding anniversary. Imagine! We've reached the

point where specialists in the field of aging talk about the
young-old and the *middle-aged-old* and the *old*-old. Just think
of that! Whether young people of A.D. 2020 will view the
elderly of their day as a bane or blessing will depend on
how we look at the elderly in our world today. And in case
it hasn't dawned on you, the elderly in A.D. 2020 is *you*. Be
sure you think about our aging nation—and an aging *you*.

How about the two-income family? That's a change. And
it would be profitable to talk about robotization and computers. I haven't said anything about political instability
across the continents and what that signals for the future.

Other changes? Medical advances, the differing political
processes of the nation, agriculture and the green revolution.
Those changes aren't the subjects that *I* choose. Every one
I've mentioned has been brought up to me by teenagers in
one place or another. Don't think they aren't paying attention. They are seeing everything. We could spend time with
each and every one of these things. We could, but we can't.
There are not enough pages in this book. However, one
more thing demands our attention.

One fundamental change is still needed: family dynamics

I recently returned from a time with teenagers in Austin,
Texas. As always, the material I presented was observations
and concerns I had gleaned from other teenagers from border to border, from coast to coast. My surest proof that
what I say is accurate is the response from the kids—attendance, applause, attention, questions. Once again, there, I
realized that the subject that gets the quickest response from
young people is parental (and family) relationships. Getting
along with mom and dad, followed by the problems of
getting along with brothers and sisters, is crucial. Let me
suggest why that is so.

Sometimes consciously, often unconsciously, teenagers
are busiest about their primary task of life: learning to trust

themselves and their own judgment. A teenager will usually develop a trusting attitude toward self whether within a family that functions in an adversary relationship or one that functions in a supportive relationship. Every family has some of both these qualities. But learning is easiest when the supporting is at a maximum and the fighting is at a minimum, when support exceeds condemnation. If the home is prisonlike, one in which parental control is total, the task the teenager faces is tougher, but he or she will grow up *anyway*. More effective and of much greater importance than the power of control is the power in affirmation and in teaching by positive example. Of course, rules and regulations are needed. We'll talk about that more in the family section, but for now two things are important: (1) We don't need nearly as many rules and regulations as we seem to generate; and (2) rules and regulations of themselves don't make great men and women. Examples do that.

We need positive homes and families. We need families that understand the value of love. This change isn't so much a change of yesterday compared to today. It is only a change of the way some families work by law versus the way a Spirit-led family lives in Christian love. This change isn't so much a matter of change that has taken place since we were kids; it's a change that *must* take place if we are to have helpful homes and healthy sons and daughters.

Summary

In this chapter I have tried to open eyes and encourage perception by stating reality. This chapter's purpose is to encourage parents to understand change so that they can better determine how to help their sons and daughters—and themselves. If you have read these words correctly, you will be comforted with the knowledge that your sons and daughters will not face the same changes as did you, nor in the same way. They will face a unique set of changes with something you didn't have—*you at their side,* ready to support and encourage and help. You can be more help to them than your parents were to you because you can model, and improve on the model, after your parents.

And the greatest good news that I could possibly have for you in this changing moment is that of the steadying reality of a God who has placed in our world a changeless Christ, a Jesus who is ". . . the same yesterday, today, and forever" (Heb. 13:8). Jesus' loving intention toward us does not vary. You won't forget that, will you? His power to give life to those of us who seek it will not change. He is so strong that he gives strength and ability to take a close, careful look at ourselves. And that's what we're going to talk about in the next chapter.

As we close this chapter, pray with me an old prayer that speaks to our present moment and need, "Create a pure heart in me, O God, and put a new and loyal spirit in me. Do not banish me from your presence; do not take your holy spirit away from me. Give me again the joy that comes from your salvation, and make me willing to obey you" (Ps. 51:10-12). I'll bet that prayer was the turning point for many an ancient parent by which they asked God to change them so they could deal positively and realistically with change. When prayed to the end, with confidence, it leaves as a parting gift one of life's greatest blessings from our God who has seen everything: *hope.* Hope in God, then hope in God's tomorrow.

2 You're Not What You Used to Be Either

The place to continue our more intensive search into the world of teens is, strange to say, not in the world of teens. It's with you and me—adults. Most specifically it is with you. As you look at teenagers, what you see and how you feel about them will depend upon where you are and what you see and feel about yourself. The more you know about "you" at this moment, the clearer will be your perspective of "them."

So let's talk about you. The chapter title is a hint of what we'll find, but let's dig it out nonetheless.

Some specific questions

By the time you become the parent of a teenager, you are likely in your 30s to mid-40s. The exact age isn't important. What *is* important is what you know about your present age, regardless of what that age may be. *Your* present age will make a difference. Whether you presently see your teenager through 35-year-old eyes or 45-year-old eyes guarantees a different perspective. But it's not their age that makes the difference, it's *your* age.

Before we go on with talk of *your* age, let's not forget the age of your marriage partner. Even if your ages are identical, your maleness or femaleness, and your individuality, will make a considerable difference in how you look at things. You are not identical.

I'm always a bit surprised by couples who come to me to talk about divorce. As I probe around I discover how little they know about each other. Maybe that's why they're talking about divorce. Had the couple been attentive to their own changes *and* those of their partner in the period leading up to their time of marital tension, things would be different.

You need to be sensitive to where you are on life's calendar, and you need to be sensitive to the chronological moment of your marriage partner. Finally, you need to be sensitive to the ways these two facts affect each other.

But let's get more specific. Let's ask the hard questions about *your* age.

What do you actually know about being 30 (or 40 or 50)? What changes have taken place in you over the past dozen years or so? Sagging jowls? A new wrinkle here or there? An unwanted bulge? Have any (all) of those changes taken place? None? What do those changes mean? Are they acceptable changes? Were they inevitable? Are there any changes that didn't have to happen—changes that you might have stopped?

What's happening on the job? (Keeping a home is a "job" too.) How are things there compared to five or ten years ago? Better? Worse? The same? Are you sure? Are you speaking only for yourself? How about your marriage partner? Are you paying an unacceptable price for achievement on the job—or nonachievement? Are your actions a result of a calculated determination of goals, or are they the inevitable consequence of vocational aimlessness? Those are tough questions, but they are crucial.

Your health—what's it like? Are you sure? Do you see a doctor regularly? Or do you operate by instinct, looking to an occasional book or newspaper column for specific information? Are there things you could or should be doing about your health? What would it take to adopt the appropriate steps that you, in your heart of hearts, know you ought to be following?

Some of you will probably find this section's questions so disturbing you will put this book down. Others will slide right by and get on to what you hope will be a more interesting part. Don't put the book down. Don't slide by. Talk to yourself. It's important that you recognize that you, like your teenage son or daughter, are in a dynamic moment of life. Both of you are in motion. This changing could create an experience that unites. Do understand that the physical changes in you and your teenager are not one of a kind. Both change physically—but the speed! Teenagers jet their way from one level of life to another. We adults move along at a more leisurely, but equally inevitable, rate. But when the day is done and the experience is over, we have both moved further down life's road. Think about that.

The sexual you

What else should we talk about? How about sex? As adults we must realize that there are very specific sexual changes taking place in our lives. These changes take place *all life long*. The changes are real. It's not as if we reach a sexual peak at 18 and begin a steady but deteriorating downhill slide from there. We're not dealing with daily sexual deterioration; we're dealing with daily sexual variation.

The specifics of sexual variation are not the same in men and women, or age by age. Men usually experience a sexual decline with the passing of later teenage years. Women generally experience just the opposite. Peaks of female sexual intensity often come in the 30s. But that's no problem. It is generally accepted that early male sexual appetites are considerably more intense and recurring than those of females. That's why male "declining" is no problem. It actually stabilizes things. The increase in a maturing wife's sexual desires match and meet the changing sexual interests of her partner. Together they ought to develop exciting new sexual adventures within the marital framework.

Don't be confused by sexual changes. They are not "good" or "bad" in themselves. Their goodness or badness will depend on what you do with them. Seek some specific information. Seek it for your good—and your partner's.

Physical changes

There's more to be said in this general area of physical change than whether we are declining or increasing. Often body strength increases with age. Increase or not, jogging, tennis, racquetball, walking, and a wide variety of competitive sports are available to all of us, regardless of our age. We can discover that some of our skills increase with age rather than decline. It still surprises me that I can hit a golf ball farther at 50 than I ever could at 20. And at 47 I ran (or made motions that approximated running) my first mile *ever*. Except in the case of severe physical disability, you can at least improve your body tone and sense of physical well-being with only a little effort. There is no inevitable rapid downhill deterioration of your physical condition—unless you let it happen.

Because your physical well-being is important in the way you relate to teens, let's pursue the question of what you could do about improving it. Join a gym. Rummage around in your town's library for books about physical change. Take a course. Attend appropriate lectures. Read some of the many magazine articles that describe the stages of life. There is *much* you can do.

Whether you agree with everything you read or are told is not important. What *is* important is that you receive information from which to draw conclusions about you and your life. Some of the information you receive will apply directly and immediately. Some will instruct you about others. Putting it all together, you must recognize that you are changing physically—and your marriage partner is changing as well. Learn all you can about these changes. If you don't, they will happen without your awareness. Then the change will only confuse you and probably scare you too!

Social/political views

Take a peek at the broad framework of social/political questions. Are you as conservative or liberal as you once were? Has your social sensitivity increased or waned? You needn't get caught up in a debate about whether you were wrong then and right now. Look for shifts and recognize them as such. You can later reflect upon the causes. Right now, spend time looking and analyzing. One thing I can state unequivocally: you have changed. You may still be the Democrat you always were, but being the Democrat-you-always-were today is different from being the Democrat-you-always-were yesterday. If that sentence doesn't make a lot of sense to you, read it again. It's true.

Your religious feelings

What about religion and your religious feelings? I am convinced that people become more religious as they mature. Do you agree?
As a much younger pastor, I assumed that folks increased in their religious sensitivity as they aged because of fear of death. I don't believe that now. I have held hands and prayed with too many dying people to have that opinion any longer. Now I believe that people get more religious as they age because they see things more clearly. From a mature perspective of themselves and those about them, they see the movement of their history *and recognize God's hand in it.* That recognition deepens their response to life and to the God who gave it. From a better perspective on the ladder of age, they perceive what they couldn't see before: they have actually been helped in Christ and strengthened in adversity by his care. And they have come to know the

source of that understanding, the Holy Spirit. They see the
Spirit as the one who brought them to faith in Jesus Christ,
their dearest and most personal friend.

I like older Christians. They seem to like themselves better
too. A lot of them get to be more fun as the calendar pages
flip by. What's happening to you in the area of your religious
feelings? As the old song asks, "Is it well with your soul?"

Your marriage and its values

One of many marriage studies indicates that when couples
fight, the cause is usually money, sex, or relatives—or a
combination of those three.

Upon closer investigation, those specific categories are
not problem areas in themselves. They are just the battlegrounds. They are the battlegrounds upon which the problem—the *real* problem—presents itself. The real problem is
about values and goals and priorities—and how a couple
relates to all of these. Specific squabbling centers on how
your marriage partner conforms in these areas to and with
you.

You and your mate develop values all your life long. The
values you had when you first married, and your understanding of them, contribute to your potential for marital
agreement or discord. The potential for either is there. If
value changes are too often hidden or denied, for whatever
reason, an explosion is almost inevitable. So it's always appropriate to ask yourself, "How have our personal values—
and values in our marriage—changed?"

If you need help in a marital evaluating process, be comforted in the knowledge that there is a lot of help out there
in the world, ready for you. There's Marriage Encounter,
for example. Marriage Encounter is a national organization
created to help good marriages become better. It helps this
happen by sensitizing husbands and wives to the needs of
each other. For more information about the organization,

ask your pastor to help you make contact with a local chapter.

Marriage Encounter, or any of the many other helpful programs available within your community, cannot by itself make a good marriage out of a bad one. No program or process can do that. Without fundamental personal change, via the work of the Holy Spirit, bad marriages can only get worse. But many of these programs help good marriages become better. They do it by improving and enhancing communication skills and the processes for sharing between marriage partners. They develop common ground between husband and wife. Marriage Encounter and other organizations encourage intimate exchange between husband and wife during the time when many changes are happening. Most people are actually surprised to discover, unknown to them, that their marriage partner has changed, and not necessarily for the worse. What a joy to realize both have changed at the same time and have rounded the same corners together—without even knowing it! If that sounds like an odd sentence, it's because it describes an odd phenomenon. People can live with each other, often very happily, without knowing very much about what's taking place in the life of the other. It's much better in the marriage when you know about the good changes (or the bad) that are taking place in your partner's life.

If your problems are beyond the help that Marriage Encounter can offer, it's time to head for professional counseling. There are professional helpers and competent marriage counselors available in every community. Even if you have to travel a great distance to find a good one, travel those miles with pleasure. The benefit you will derive from the effort exerted will be worth it.

It all adds up

It should come as no surprise to any of us that there is a direct relationship between an overall sense of well-being, mental attitude, and physical condition. All three are inter-connected. All three are, in different ways, related to age. It is imperative that you study your specific age. In your study you will see yourself more clearly. Ultimately, from this better perspective, you will see new truths about your teenager too.

Can't people see?

Why can't people see the changes for themselves? Why do we need to talk about change? Who in the world would want to deny the reality and effect of personal change?

Believe me, the number of those who deny change is myriad. Some who deny change haven't fully come to grips with their own sinful nature and do not understand the grace of God. They must, of necessity, resist all talk about change. They wouldn't know what to do with it, whether good or bad. What other path is open to them but one of denial?

Deniers move through life like Sherman tanks. Unaffected by events or circumstances, they plow on into their tomor-rows ignoring everything that is going on around them. People like that will not visit a professional counselor, or meet with a group, or confront the truth. For them, the only final change that is tolerable is a changed partner, or a changed job, or a changed city. But the joke is on them. *They always bring the same old person along wherever they go and with whomever they unite.* Their denial of change forces their history to repeat itself.

Jesus Christ, change, and the new potential

Those of us who know Christ as more than a teacher—who accept him as Lord and Savior and sin bearer—are considerably more open to the reality of change than others might be. Why? We're not smarter, but we have a way of dealing with mistakes and flaws and errors that beats denial. We take our sinful humanity, put it at the foot of the cross, and there leave it, along with the consequences of all that we have done and are. Christ forgives us and shows us how to forgive—ourselves and others. In that action, we prepare for something new.

Christians use the term *new* in so many different ways. We even have a language of the "new"—words like *regeneration* and *repentance* and *renewal*. Those words connect to ideas like *being born again, having a new mind,* and *turning around* 180 degrees to reverse our course. That's why Christians dote on change. Change is at the very heart of the Christian understanding of progress. A changed Moses, a changed David, a changed Paul, a changed Peter, and a changed Jacob confronted their changed moments with their changed lives.

Once you nail down the *possibility* of change in your life through Christ, and then further nail down the *probability* of change in your life in Christ, and then finally nail down the *inevitability* of change in your life with Christ, you are ready to accept that same potential in others. You will come to the conviction that your spouse *can change.* You will also know that your teenage sons and daughters *can change.*

As I write these words, I remember promising my wife years ago, in one of her more distraught moments, that our children actually would not head off to the first grade sucking their thumbs, wearing diapers, and dragging their quilts behind them. On the darker days in those early years, I don't think she believed me. But because I believed in change (and down deep so did she), the portrait of hope that I painted was at least comforting. My prophecies all came true. All of our children changed—and for the better too.

Christian change is just as assured as the changes in our children. Christ does his promised work wherever he is allowed. Ask for his power!

Change in you—and in your teenager too

When we as parents actually understand that we have changed, when we realize both how difficult and tedious that change can be, when we are sensitive to the painfulness of that process, then we can better grasp the impact change has upon those who are less experienced than we are. I'm referring to our teenage sons or daughters.

Teenagers have a tough time with change. They have a limited history of its possibility. That's because they are young. They can suffer incredible depressions. That's because they care. In depression (based on hopelessness), they attempt suicide with such tragic frequency that it is the number two cause of death among the young. Teenagers can develop stress ulcers and experience powerful emotional pressures. When we look at them from our parental mountaintop of recognized change, our hearts go out and our caring reaches to those who are so busily moving out of their childhood into the totally new experience of being grown-ups. They are walking the same kind of road of change we do, with one frightening difference: they have fewer inner supports. If change is tough for us, it's tougher for them. At the very least, we adults should pressure young people less and listen to them more.

The power of example and tenderness

Once we acknowledge change as inevitable, it is hoped we will sense the limited value of pressure, force, and punishment in changing others. Intimidation, coercion, public shamings, embarrassing punishments, and unreasonable demands do not strengthen and improve a teenager—or anyone else. Those things make people mad. That's what St. Paul meant when he said, "the law brings down . . . anger . . ." (Rom. 4:15). Unless the law is understood in the greater context of the gospel, and administered in an evangelical, balanced mix of law *and* gospel, all the law finally does is toughen your son or daughter to the point that they are insulated against you and can hardly wait for the moment to escape your dominance.

Understanding the weakness of force and its assured inevitable failure urges us to cast around for an alternative. Behold! There it is! *The power of example.* The power of example comes packaged in the useful method of soft, sensitive, and sensible answers.

Knowing the power of example and the strength of tenderness helps you bide your time in difficult moments. You can wait until you are asked for help. You don't have to burst into the life of a son or daughter with unsolicited, unwanted, and ultimately unacceptable advice. The kids will come to those who live Christ—and who wait.

Does that mean that we as Christians don't have rules in our homes? Does that mean that a parent can't give an opinion? Of course not. Christians are not lawless people. We have "rules." We understand the law for what it really is. We know that "rules" can be used to explain. And that's about all. Rules don't change anybody. They only curb irresponsible outbursts! Change happens differently. Change happens through example, and the Spirit's movement. If you're not quite sure how to deal with rules, use this rule: treat your sons or daughters as if they were your friends. Do for your teenager what you'd do for your best friend— and in a friendly way too!

As a specific example on how this works, let me pose a question. Would you stand idly by if a dear friend were doing something you knew would be hurtful or potentially injurious to himself or to others? Of course not. But your approach would be controlled, restrained, loving, and careful. Right? You would earnestly strive to use language that would improve communication. You would woo your friend and hope, in the tenderness of your approach, to win.

I always use the same criteria in dealing with daughters or sons. Treat them as friends. They are more than friends; they are your flesh and blood, in biblical language, "bone of your bone." I don't need to encourage you to love them, do I? Be what you want them to be, and correct them with firm tenderness. Clear?

One more time

So what do we have now that we're near the end of this chapter? We have a home that has at least three changing people in it. There's a mom changing in her own female/wife/mother ways. There's a dad changing in his own male/husband/father ways. There's a teenager changing in his or her own unique and rapid young adult way. Begin with that.

Second, there is a need to claim the similarities of the experiences all three are facing. All are in a changing process. All are facing a new now.

Third, all need each other. Parents must never forget that teens can, and do, teach. Parents ought acknowledge this and develop opportunities for this teaching to happen. If children should be seen and not heard (and where in Scripture is that said?), then teenagers—who are not children—should be seen *and* heard. They can be God's special and specific gifts to parents to help them through tough and trying times.

One of the tenderest moments in my talks before teen groups is when I try to explain to them their personal role in their families. I ask them whether they have ever wondered why God put them into their specific homes. Did God choose ideal parents for them and then make the connection? Or, I ask them, could it be possible that God in heaven put them into households where their parents were in such desperate need of help that *only* a young person of their potential could lead these oldsters to safety? It gets very quiet when I turn the tables of perception in this way and force them to react to a God-given role that recognizes spiritual accountability to the Lord—by teenagers. I always admire the seriousness with which they receive these new thoughts and the eagerness with which they claim them as their own.

Am I talking rubbish? Is the concept presented in the last paragraph outlandish and impossible? When you've seen enough homes, you realize that in thousands of them the "oldest" and the most "responsible" person present is often little more than a dozen years old—and some of the most immature are well past 40. Homes that offer the greatest hope will treasure every resource God has given them regardless of the chronological age of the blessing.

Finally, you've caught the sense of this chapter if you recognize that you and your teenager are both changing—dramatically, absolutely, irrevocably, and inevitably. Parents and teenagers are in the same boat. That ought to say something to you. Don't punch holes in the other end of your boat (their end) while trying to explain that you're letting the rising water out. You will soon discover that your actions will result in a severe sogginess at your end as well. It doesn't have to be that way. With tenderness and care, you can minister to one another. As you stand in awe of the incredible beauty of life that God gives to each of us, you can praise him for every other person in your household. And you can praise God for each day he gives and the changes that come with each dawn.

Don't be afraid of change in yourself. Don't be afraid of change in others. Don't be ignorant about either. Strive to know and understand what change means. If you are willing to exert that energy, you are ready to move on. And we now will—to mystifying but myriad meaningless myths. If you can tolerate the pun, we'll concentrate on *mythtakes* about teenagers.

3 Myths about Teenagers —Clearing the Air

In *Thank God I Am a Teenager* (Augsburg, 1976), Dr. Bardill and I wrote a chapter titled "Don't You Believe It." In that chapter we listed many of the myths that teenagers have to confront about themselves. Judging from the response we received from thousands of young people, the list was found useful.

What facts do you know about teenagers? Do you recognize the myths? Can you identify the distortions about teenagers that we all carry? Do you know what's true—or not true—about your sons or daughters and their teenage friends?

In this chapter we're going to concentrate upon things that are not true about teenagers. We'll try to nail down the lies for the lies they are. Let's start out.

Myth one: the teenage years are a period of severe personality maladjustment.

Dr. Bardill first surprised me when he showed me a study of high school teachers interviewed a few years ago. Eighty percent of those specialists in young people were convinced that the teens are a period of severe personality maladjustment. That perception is so patently untrue, and provably so, that one wonders how trained educators could be so very wrong.

I suppose the answer is that they are human and subject to the same misconceptions as the rest of us. Aren't high school kids in literature and on TV portrayed as warped in a wide variety of ways? I suppose that writers for television would defend their portrayals by claiming that there is not much demand for TV series about nice young men and women who flow from a pleasant adolescence to a full-fledged and well-adjusted adulthood without many crises. Yet, thank God, that's what usually happens. Most young people pass through their teens unscathed and unscarred, excited about the possibilities of their tomorrows.

In specific, there are studies that show that 75% of all teenagers adjust to their daily new experiences with ease and suffer minimal tension through it all. While one-quarter have *some* difficulty, only a small fraction suffer from anything that might remotely be called a severe personality maladjustment. Yet that smallest fraction is the type most generally featured in dramas, remembered best from books, portrayed most clearly on TV.

There are many adjustments in the teenage years and a lot of changes to be experienced. Some of them take place at dizzying speed. But many more than most young people move from challenge to challenge, from change to change, from choice to choice, with little difficulty. Severe personality maladjustments are not normal for teenagers. Change is. Don't confuse the two.

Myth two: it's best to grow up as speedily as possible

What do you think about that one? Is it best to press for indications of maturity as fast as you can? I don't think so. It seems God doesn't think so either.

Compared to the overall maturation rate of animals, man matures at a much more leisurely pace. It should seem obvious that the Lord didn't intend the growing process to be hurried, hustled, or hastened. No one thinks that a cake can be baked in half the time if the oven is set at twice the recommended heat. There are things that, if they are to be done right, simply take time. Developing a teenager and helping him or her through the early phases of young adulthood is one such task.

It's comforting to know that most of the business of growing up happens at a kind of universal, preordained speed. It also has a certain inevitable quality about it. The only people I can think of who don't finally make it to some recognizable level of adulthood are either damaged en route or are personally determined to *not* arrive. Many of those, in either category, are finally placed in institutions of one type or another. But for the rest, growing up is an orderly, unhurried, sequential, step-by-step experience that starts around 12 and essentially continues through the balance of life. The early-blooming Brooke Shields of this world are not to be envied. For whatever reasons, they skipped (or skipped through) a very important stage of God's intention for them. Those who do manage to hurry through that phase of growing up without severe difficulties (and as you read about "them," see how often that happens) do so almost accidentally.

The key to a pleasant journey through the teenage years is *pacing*. Parents can do a lot to help orderly and pleasant pacing happen. They can keep the focus on the natural and usual process of maturing. They can consistently acknowledge the existence and the advantages of a steady development. Being *first* with a bra, *first* to date alone, *first* to have a paper route is not the stuff out of which lasting useful lessons inevitably develop. Many of us "late bloomers" haven't done too badly in life.

This whole business of pacing and orderly development makes me think of a few young mothers who boast about the early age their sons are potty-trained. The only thing that actually takes place is that there is a maternal recognition of that "look," after which the mothers hustle their Henrys to the throne. No big deal. All the other kids ultimately learn how to potty by themselves—without mother's desperate searching for some sign of the child's superiority. A few just couldn't let their kids handle one of life's earliest learning experiences by themselves. Too bad for mothers—and sons.

So, are good parents interested in helping young people grow? Sure! Should they be interested in helping them grow up fast and first? Why? Teens lack significant adult skills and experiences. They must develop the first and await the latter. When surrounded by modeled maturity, teens absorb it easily and effectively—but at their own rate. Teenagers will enjoy the growing process, and bless you for your part in it, if you give them room and opportunity to sprout at their own speed.

Myth three: constant conflict between parents and teenagers is normal

There's nothing normal about *constant* conflict, no matter who it's between. Constant conflict indicates a problem. Get help. The fact is that the overwhelming majority of kids do not constantly squabble with their parents. There isn't perpetual tension and deep-seated animosity in the relationship either. Most love and respect their moms and dads, hold them in high esteem, and seek to serve them—just as the Fourth Commandment encourages.

Strange to say, when there is conflict present, it can actually be initiated by the parent for reasons that have nothing to do with the son or daughter and are in no way related to them. Sometimes parents stir up the pot because they're getting older and think they need some reaffirmation. When that reaffirmation is sought through dominance (remember what we said about the law in the last chapter?), it will backfire. And there will be conflict.

However, not all conflict is malicious or intentional or negative. Everybody in the house is experiencing growing pains. Peace and tranquility ultimately come, but they come through a process of inner searching, experimentation in communication with one another, and in the joyful discovery that the best relationship between a parent and teen carries the common name of friendship. Learning those truths are not all bad. The process can be quite exciting.

But constant fighting? If that's the case, you ought to do something about it. And you can.

Myth four: teenagers and parents can't communicate

For some teenagers and parents, that's plainly not true. They have worked hard at developing the necessary skills, and they practice those communication skills with intensity. Others of us need lessons.

The lesson that most of us need is a lesson in listening. It shouldn't surprise us that listening is the key to communication. If you can clearly hear what the other is saying, the possibility of useful response improves dramatically.

The communication process is also significantly enhanced if we are able to do some careful historical comparing. (Remember Chapter 1?) I work hard at honestly comparing what life was like when I was younger with what life is like today. It helps me understand kids today. It helps me understand myself.

For example, I've sought permission to watch a grade school in action on a normal day. What an eye opener! It's not like it used to be! I won't argue whether it's better or worse. For communication's sake, I only need to realize that it's not the way it used to be. When I evaluate the differences, I know so much more than I did before. Many of the things (most of the things) are the same. A few of the things (and they are often the most obvious) are different. While not every change is an improvement, not every variation is a deteriorating reality either.

Time invested in a careful comparing (schools, clothes, magazines, privileges, etc.) can pay incredible dividends. It helps me understand today's young people better. As I describe the changes to my younger friends, it helps them understand me a little better too.

If I'm careful in how I speak, I can help teenagers as they travel from where they are to where I am (or where we both ought to be) in the least complicated and most helpful fashion possible. Because I want to do that, I recognize that communication skills are critical. The better the communication, the less the conflict. See how myths three and four relate? Chapter 6 will help people who recognize the relationship and want help.

Myth five: young people today are not as moral as they used to be

Do you believe that? Most people seem to. I sure don't. Some parents keep forgetting that there were Florence Crittenden Homes for unwed mothers when they were young. I was surprised when a specialist in drug usage told me that the highest percentage of drug addiction in the history of the United States was in 1918. How could that be? Simple. Most of the patent medicine of that time was so laced with narcotics and opiates that users were inevitably on a perpetual jag.

Alcohol is now a severe problem. Yesterday too! What do you think prohibition was all about? Murder. Rape. Red light districts. Crime. Delinquency. There was plenty of all of that in the past. Read any newspaper. Search through historical documents. The facts are clear. The texture of life today is no worse than it was yesterday.

But there is something that is radically different about today's moral moment compared with yesterday's. I was shielded. Weren't you? I believe the average teenager today is confronted with more specific temptation before noon than I faced through my entire high school years. If that's an exaggerated statement, then it's only mildly so.

I stand in awe at the temptations today's adult-run society places before teens. In our yearning to maintain constitutional safeguards, we permit an inexcusable pressuring on young people that boggles the mind. Teens are surrounded by filth, immorality, and decadence. Most handle it just fine. Many teens chart a course of decency in the midst of all that immorality that their parents should emulate. But it's sad that our young people are forced to grow up in a society where what their parents know to be wrong surrounds them in every moment—an adult-operated society that they did not make but that they must deal with. I wonder what that says about those of us who are older. I know what it says about teenagers. It says they are terrific!

Those are five of the distortions that Dr. Bardill and I discovered and presented to teenagers some years ago. But they are not the only distortions that parents must consider. I'd like to list a heavy half-dozen (that means seven) distortions that have been brought to my attention by young people, and their parents, since that earlier list was prepared. We'll just call them "additional myths."

Additional myth one: teenagers are all alike

I use the term *teenager* as a generalized category, but I don't think I ever make the mistake of dealing with any specific young person in a generalized way. Each of our four children was a teenager in some very importantly different ways. Paracelsus offered these words of considerable wisdom: "Whoever thinks that all fruits ripen at the same rate as grapes knows nothing about strawberries." That makes sense to me. What it really tells me when applied to teenagers is that each youngster is different.

Each oldster is different too. I do my best to help young people think about their moms every once in a while as

"Marcie" or "Jo" or whatever name their dads use. They need to realize that within their moms is tucked away another very special person who is best known and most clearly described as Marcie or Jo or whatever her name is. That person has unique qualities, unique needs, unique hopes, and undergoes a kind of unique suffering like unto no other human being. She needs to be treasured within those specific blessings and burdens that she bears or brings. Do you like that thought? I do. So do the kids. Teenagers ought to be seen in the same way.

Additional myth two: the teens are not a period of turmoil

That's not the same as saying that teens are not a phase of severe personality maladjustments or a period of conflict. I'm talking less about the young people and more about the outside influences on their lives.

There *is* a lot of turmoil going on during the teens. That turmoil can't and shouldn't be glossed over. But much of that turmoil has at least one other dimension: it's normal to life. Job said it: "Man brings trouble on himself, as surely as sparks fly from a fire" (Job 5:7).

Let me illustrate what I mean. Acne is turmoil. Menstruation is turmoil. Self-consciousness and awkwardness are turmoil. Physical plainness is turmoil. Ignorance about social skills is turmoil. But all that turmoil is easily controllable. It can be turned around—advantageously.

Acne keeps a lot of kids unattractive at a time in their lives when they aren't ready to handle what it means to be attractive. Right? Isn't menstruation a monthly reminder of femininity and fertility and sexuality, and doesn't it offer a forced moment for reflecting upon those things and what they could mean? Plainness, self-consciousness, minimal social skills are the stuff out of which growth takes place, *if effort is exerted.*

Each of the cited turmoils (and so many others) can be turned into a positive moment in the hands of the caring parent.They are superb subjects for discussion and sharing. They are the specifics that are integral to the teenage experience. Out of each exciting perception a new understanding can develop.

Don't be discouraged if your teenager doesn't always see the positive potential of the point you want to make. That's why you are the teacher and why they are under parental care. So teach, teacher! Help them to learn with you standing at their side. T-U-R-M-O-I-L may be just another way of spelling T-O-G-E-T-H-E-R-N-E-S-S.

Additional myth three: teenagers are irresponsible

I surely don't believe that. While I do realize that responsibility is not a natural instinct, I am stunned by how very responsible teenagers generally are.

Others disagree with that myth, citing teenagers who don't clean their rooms as prime examples. From the volume of mail on that subject, I would guess that dirty rooms cause more tension in normal homes than anything else. But is a dirty room a sign of irresponsibility?

At a gathering of parents and teenagers, I waded into this subject of cleaning rooms. I asked everyone (parents and kids alike) to see themselves as teenagers for the moment. Then, from that perspective, I asked them to help me list what a teenager might be "saying" with a dirty room.

You wouldn't believe it! We found over 30 messages. One was "It's the only way I can get attention." Another, "I'm angry at my mother and this is how I get back at her." Yet another, "If you won't clean up my air by not smoking, I won't make your house livable by cleaning my room."

Than I turned the tables and asked everyone to assume the role of parent. Again we made a list. The list was just as long. When it was all over, most agreed that while some kids might have a dirty room because they are lazy and irresponsible, the majority are trying to send a message that they can't seem to get through in any other way. I'm not sure they're getting through any better this way, but we who are older need to understand the process and make sure it has a proper name. That name *isn't* irresponsibility.

I once shared a hotel at a youth gathering with more than a thousand young people who were in residence there for a weekend, together with a number of other guests. Halfway through the gathering, an incredible snowstorm struck. At dawn, the manager discovered that he had all these kids, many other guests, and no way for the day crew to get to work. No cooks. No cleaning people. No bellhops. No maintenance folks. On their own, the teenagers took over. They made sure that an investment of millions of dollars and the safety and well-being of thousands of people were protected until help got there. What do you think of that? On a smaller scale, it happens every day.

I don't think teenagers are irresponsible. *They can be.* But if they're irresponsible, it's usually at the same level and frequency as the adults around them.

Additional myth four: teenagers like to spend a lot of time alone

That's not true. Not unless they are forced to. Not unless no one will talk with them.

There are times when they will want to be away from parents and family. There are times when they will want to go to their rooms, listen to their radios or records; times when they will want to think privately. Private moments are important to life. But so is community time, especially when that community is the family.

Kids usually go off by themselves when there is no one to talk to in their homes. Embarrassing studies of conversation in Christian homes consistently surface the same strange things. The studies show that there is very little conversation in the home. Of what there is, much is abrupt.

Not much love gets expressed. Among the more commonly expressed thoughts in a Christian home are things like: "Take out the trash." "Turn out the lights." "Go to bed." "Shut the door." Very little "I love you!" Sound familiar?

My first instinct is to say that those studies are not true. Then I close my mouth and open my ears. I quickly discover how truthful they are. But why?

As I mentioned in Chapter 1, a number of years ago I interviewed teenagers on TV week after week. I discovered young people talk most comfortably about four subjects: school, music, boys and girls, and sports. You can validate that list easily by driving a group of teenagers somewhere and listening as they talk in the backseat. As they grow older, their span of conversational subjects will expand considerably. But in the early years, as teenagers are learning how to converse, those are the subjects they handle best. They don't talk much with oldsters because we seldom meet them at the point of their expertise.

So why not meet them there? Talk with your teenagers in the subject areas they are most comfortable. Make sure that you are in conversation, not delivering a lecture. Make sure you listen at least as much as you talk. Try to learn. The result of that effort, expended over a longer period of time, will be fewer hours with you standing in the kitchen while a son or daughter with whom you would love to talk is closeted in his or her room. The separation is not because they don't want to be with you; it is generally the result of an inability of parent and child to carry on a decent conversation.

Additional myth five: teenagers have no money

People who sell products to teenagers—jeans, tapes, records, and stereo sets—know that's not true. They know just how much money kids have.

I don't know of a single study of teenage economics that doesn't conclude that they have more disposable income than any other members of their families. (Disposable income is a term to describe the money that is still available after a person has taken care of all life's demanding obligations.)

Recognizing that kids have some money, some parents try to use that fact as a vehicle for teaching monetary responsibility. We urge them to save money for college or a car or for something else they want. In that way we teach them thrift, the value of work, and the value of a goal in life. Or do we?

Often all we're teaching them is selfishness. We teach them to *save for themselves* and compliment them for it. But who of us actually teaches money management? Who makes sure our teenagers understand the biblical view of generosity, charity, and care for others? *Those* are the areas where difficulties develop later in life. Because we don't fully understand the potential of the moment and don't always recognize our responsibility as teachers, we have a tendency to raise kids who have a lot of money and who don't know how to give to anyone. Many of them don't even know they're supposed to.

In premarital counseling, I usually ask young couples whether they have ever given a total of $200 in cash or gifts to any one person in all their lives. I don't care what the relationship might be to the person to whom they may have given it; that doesn't make any difference.

Only occasionally have they given that much to anyone. Not to brother. Not to sister. Not to mom or dad. Not to anyone. They are trained to save and keep and get and store and bank—for themselves.

What a shock when a young man who has been trained to look out for himself marries a young woman who has been trained to look out for herself! Each enters marriage eager to receive and totally inexperienced in giving. Yet nothing in married life works well (not sex, not family, not vocation, not goals, not conversation, not protection, not care) that isn't built on giving. Giving *first*. That's why it's important for us to realize that teenagers do have an awful lot of money, and to recognize that we must show them how to be responsible and responsive givers with their bucks. Help them learn how to give even if they give away some of their precious college money. The lesson they will learn for life in so doing is greater than anything Harvard or Yale could ever teach them.

Additional myth six: the teenage years are idyllic, filled with free time

Just test it out. I dare you. Write out the daily schedule of your teenager. Don't evaluate it, write it. List the time-consuming obligations he or she has. Total up the hours for school, for meetings, for travel, for work, for study, for satisfying social necessities, for church, for family, and the like.

I've done this diarying with many young people and have invariably been astonished at the complex schedule teenagers must satisfy and the time demands they must meet. I'm convinced that the average teenager has more obligations and responsibilities day by day than the average adult. Teens are busy. They have many commitments. Recognize that and help teens meet them.

Additional myth seven: for parents, the sooner the teen years are over the better

I suppose that's true for some. Those who insist on staying awake whenever one of their kids is out at night will conclude that the teen years were a miserable experience. They missed a lot of sleep.

If parents insist on living through every experience that their sons or daughters face, anticipating all the potentially frightful misadventures; if they hover over their youngsters and feel they must make each decision for them; if that's what it's like at your house, then I believe the teen years are going to be an absolutely miserable time—for mom and dad. To compound the misery, if we act this way, when our teens are old enough, they'll leave us. And they'll never look back!

God didn't mean for us to live our teenagers' lives. We have our own lives to live. To make sure we understand this, God sent us all the message of the umbilical cord. As soon as your child is born, by God's creative intention, the umbilical cord is cut. In that moment an independent and new support system takes over. Some of what is needed by the child is still provided by the parents. Most of what is required, the children must supply themselves. No more direct-tubed food from mom. No more pleasant protection in the womb. Babies must learn to suck and breathe and rest and fight fevers and walk and avoid open fires for themselves.

Oh, yes, there is a continued place for parents. We are to teach, support, and guide. But when all is said and done, that's about all we can do. Once that's pretty well done (around the age of 12 or 13), the best thing to do is go to bed and get some sleep.

The parent who best makes it through the teenage years is the one who understands the difference between preparation and separation. The first 12 years of life are a time of parental preparation. The next 7 to 10 years are for applying principles for living in separation. Teens practice theirs. Parents practice theirs. That's God's way.

It's exciting to view the teen years with that understanding. It's exciting to see our role in the preparation of our children as both teenager and parent work toward the goal of separation. That's God's plan. Once we understand God's system, we can relax. We are to do all the things we are supposed to do. We don't have to do the things we're not supposed to do. That's not too complicated, is it?

When your sons and daughters feel as free as God intends them to be, a whole new dimension of relationship develops.

Parents were never intended to be pals to little children; they are to be loving moms or dads. But being a pal is a rather appropriate relationship for later in life. If you handle the teenage years well, you can become fast friends with your sons or daughters. The trust awarded to parents in later years is shaped by the way they handle the earlier ones.

There's a lot more that could be said about *mythtakes*. (There I go again!) I believe I've given enough clues to help you make it on your own with others that surface from time to time. This chapter was intended to clear away much of the distortion and faulty folklore that many folks accept as truth. Don't be guilty of that. Use your eyes. See what you see. Plug into the Word of God. Study the great model: our heavenly Father who shows us what parenting is all about by his treatment of his dear children on earth. In the Father's example and through the Spirit's guidance, you can bless your children who happen to be teenagers right now. And, if you treat them appropriately, they will most assuredly be your good friends tomorrow. That's no myth.

This chapter is now history for us. What's next? If the myths needed deflating (and they did), then the facts need elevating (and they do). It's time to focus on facts. In the next chapter we look at teenagers and teenaging and the truth about both.

4 Facts about Teenagers— The Crucial Tip of the Iceberg

Having laughed at the lies about kids and exposed the myths of the teen years in the last chapter, we still have quite a task before us. Just as Chapter 2 asked how much we knew about ourselves, this chapter is going to ask how much we know about our teenage sons or daughters.

As a sort of pop quiz, let me start with this: if you were to write down every fact you knew about teenagers and the teenage period, how many pages could you fill? Facts, now—not impressions or misty memories. A page?

In this chapter I'll present basic information about teenagers. Facts. (Well, maybe a little opinion added in here and there.) After we study the facts, we'll be in a better position to understand our younger friends—and ourselves.

Here's a quickie insight to begin with: the teen years last from the tail end of 12 until the first day of 20. Seven full years. That's a fact. That's about as long as the president of the United States will serve, assuming he or she is given a second term. Seven years is getting close to a decade. No modern war lasted in its fullest fury for seven years. It took less than that for our nation to put a man on the moon after President Kennedy gave us the challenge. Seven years. A long time? Depends. A lot happens in those seven years.

It's at least a long enough time for all the important things to take place.

From the idea of seven years—seven *long* years—it's only a short step to the subject of *spacing*. *Spacing* is a lot like the *pacing* of the last chapter, but still different. By spacing I mean that not everything has to be done overnight, or before fall, or by the time a teen is 15. Since the teen years last such a long time, the speed at which and spacing with which things are done is very important.

If everything that needs to be learned during the teen years is left to the last minute of the 19th year, things will get compressed into a mighty tight ball of activity. But if the teens are seen as an extended period, much of the pressure to "get it done" can be relieved. We can settle down to doing things at God's more leisurely pace.

So there you have a couple of facts about the teen years. But there are a lot more.

Three segments

Hard on the heels of our observations about the length of the teenage era and spacing is another elementary and important insight: the teen years come in segments. Most young people find their segments boundaried by graduations.

The first segment (called the *early teens*) extends from grade school graduation through the ninth or tenth grade. The next segment (appropriately tagged the *middle teens*) extends from the tenth through the twelfth grade. The third segment (you guessed it—the *late teens*) spins off toward 20 after starting at the end of high school.

Recognizing the existence of segmentation and the respective boundaries is important. Distinct changes take place within, and occasionally across, the segmented periods. If you understand the segments, you'll have a better chance at understanding the changes.

Parents are often caught unaware by segmentational shiftings. They figure that once they have a problem solved somewhere around age 13 it ought to last to 20. No such luck.

Three questions

Not only are there segments, but each segment has its own dominant question. The question of the first segment is, "Who am I going to be?" Imitation, submission to peer pressure, and a marked, but understandable, lack of self-confidence are all part of this early moment. Are there any groups more clannish and cliquish than junior high school students? This condition may not be justifiable, but it makes sense.

The second stage asks a more contemplative question: "Who am I now?" High school English teachers will tell you that many kids at this stage write penetrating essays and wonderfully personal and poignant poetry and demonstrate a surprisingly reflective approach to their circumstances. This period can be intensely emotional and even somewhat mercurial, but that's all part of the phase. It's during this time, while parents talk about puppy love, that kids recognize this emotion for what it really is: their first love. For quite a few, their first love is also their last love. Once discovered, teenage love *can* last a lifetime! Make you nervous? Be careful how you talk about your grandchild's father—or mother!

The third segment digs into the question, "Who was I?"—hoping that the conclusion will be a springboard for future progress and additional personal growth. You've heard the expression "sophomoric wisdom," right? The sophomore it's talking about is the college sophomore who, at 20, is wiser than he'll ever be. He really believes he can answer the third segment's question definitively. His answer lasts—for a while.

Many areas of change

These three segments are marked, not only by inner churnings and intellectual shiftings, but by distinct physical changes as well. For instance, during the three phases much happens to any boy. During the earliest segment, a boy's muscle strength will double. He is twice as strong at 16 as he was at 12. And that strengthening continues thereafter until, at 20, his is an adult body. The muscle is not just a matter of mass. It's a matter of what he can do for himself and what he can do to make sure others don't force him into a position against his will. Muscle strength has a lot to do with how you get along—or don't get along—with other people. Muscle strength, in turn, is related to those three segments.

Girls experience physical changes too! During the teens, a young lady's "baby fat" starts to disappear. In its place, attractive curves become apparent and outline the mature female figure. In addition, girls, too, grow in strength and develop physical dexterity during this three-segment period.

By the way, do you know that boys and girls develop coordination skills at different times during their lives? Girls are first. That's why girls like to dance in junior high and boys generally don't. Makes sense. Why would a gawky boy want to dance with a graceful girl? All of that will change later.

During these wonderful teenage times, both boys and girls become conscious of their sexual selves and experience pleasant, but confusing, physical sensations. They'd like some straight talk about sex, sexuality, sexual intercourse, and other aspects of this important subject. It is in the expectation that parents will make the appropriate explanations to their sons and daughters that God surrounds teenagers with families during this crucial period of their lives. How are you doing? Are you interpreting and explaining what's happening to them? That's a parental responsibility. It's a parental opportunity too.

One of the most exciting things that takes place in teen-agers takes place within their heads—in their minds. The teens—by themselves—are a mind-expanding experience—literally! During the teen years, young men and women learn how to conceptualize. That means they learn how to work out things in their minds and resolve intricate problems in their heads. Simultaneously they are developing the skills of logical evaluation. Often as a companion aspect of mind-expanding discoveries, they will start saying that they like school—for the first time. Many times they're unable or unwilling to publicly claim this shift, but if you watch closely, you'll see the changes.

A chance for you

All teenagers want to learn to do things at which they can excel or at which they achieve success. Some demon-strate amazing early abilities for understanding computers or cars or games or audio systems or other technical aspects of modern life. Smart parents have a great chance to "meet" their sons or daughters at these points of increasing teenage excellence. Teenagers usually describe their newfound skills as fun. Of course it's fun! Superior achievement and exciting new experiences coupled together with unanticipated ad-ventures are always fun. You can be part of their fun, if you want.

That's still not all. Broad-based social sensitivity increases during the teen years as well. What a pushover high school kids are for anyone with a sad story! It's great watching them spot a community problem, claim it as their own, and commit themselves to a solution. They give it their all. Sel-dom will they quit short of success! For instance, have you noticed how teens will "walk" for almost every disease in the dictionary? Or gather money, canned goods, or clothing for about every hard-luck family that comes along? They sell for causes they think are genuine, visit sick and elderly when there appears to be a need, and expend great love and attention to the unattended or handicapped children. In their spare time they develop genuine anger over ignored social problems.

Most of us can remember when teenagers (and others barely out of the teen ages) helped reshape United States foreign policy and our national stance on Vietnam. The kids said no to the government's yes. A few years before that, teenagers had a lot to do with reordering our national perceptions about race. The young normally lead the way on social issues that affect women, the aged, the handicapped, and others who need help.

Take a good look at *all* that is happening in your teenager's life. At first glance it may look placid. A closer inspection shows that it is excitingly vibrant. There's a place for you too.

Let's get specific

But what specifically concerns teenagers? Instead of giving you my opinion, I'll let teenagers talk to you through me. I've received thousands of letters and notes from young people over the years. A more thorough development of the sections that follow is presented in *Getting Along* (Augsburg, 1980), a book that I wrote based on what teenagers had shared with me.

There are five primary issues and concerns that dominate their sharings. In time I discovered that the five issues I informally surfaced with them closely parallel the results of other formal surveys conducted among young people of every religious denomination and in every part of the nation.

Number one—themselves

Their number one concern? Understandably, *themselves*. They list a lengthy sequence of things that make them happy or that they perceive as serious personal problems. That list contains everything from acne to awkwardness, from over-weight to underachievement, from peer popularity to parental abuse. And the list goes on and on in an almost endless recitation, with this common denominator: it focuses on themselves.

Why such broad-ranged yet intense personal concern? In a society that does very little to affirm its young people (and you may feel it does even less in affirming parents), teenagers develop a lot of confused perceptions about themselves. Most of them are negative. These negative opinions, left unattended, turn into monstrous distortions—so monstrous that one of the major causes of death among teenagers is suicide. Can you believe that?

How can bright, sensitive, and caring young people feel so desperate about their personal conditions that they are driven to take their own lives? This is not the place to dwell on that question, but this is the place where it must be acknowledged. Many young people have an intensely negative viewpoint about themselves. All young people have a moderately negative self-perception.

Treatment centers for helping teenagers are available in almost every community. Few of them are long-term facilities. Long-term treatment for most kids isn't needed. Most need a brief period of high-powered reinforcement and a lot of love and reassurance to get back on track. They want that help and accept it eagerly, *if it is available* and if parents will support them.

Unbelievably, I find one of the greatest obstacles in getting assistance to teenagers is parents who refuse to heed their youngsters' cries for help. Getting help for your teenager is not the same as admitting you are a poor parent. And, if it were, what's the difference? Would you deny your youngster assistance rather than stain your image as a parent? Some would. Fortunately, most will not.

If you have any questions about your teenager, if someone with professional competence is suggesting they need specialized help, if you have a sneaking suspicion that things are beyond your control, don't resist the inclination to seek assistance. Have an evaluation made of your teenager by one or two professionals. Then you and your son or daughter can make a decision of what to do based upon professionally ascertained evidence.

There's no good reason why most teenagers should have a poor self-image, but many do. Help change that fact!

Number two—their parents

Right behind teenagers' concern for personal needs comes a barrelful of questions about relationships with their parents. They ask all kinds of questions. They want to know why fathers yell, why parents drink to excess at home, why adults have trouble saying I love you. They ask about communication with their folks, questions of privacy and personal rights, unreasonable parental expectations. They are concerned about the lack of trust they experience and a whole span of other things. As the years have passed, I still get the same kind of notes, letters, and comments. These concerns haven't changed.

Remember, the young people I contact are not society's rejects. They haven't opted out of life! They came into contact with me either through my writings or at some church gathering. They care enough to express their concerns by note or letter. They seek a discussion. *These* are the ones who are asking such penetrating questions about family and parental concerns.

We'll deal more with the question on how to handle these intrafamily concerns in later chapters, especially the one dealing with communication and problem solving. For the moment, accept it as a fact: the events in the home are heavy on the hearts of young Christian teenagers.

Number three—others who live in their homes

Their third area of concern is brothers, sisters—and grandmothers. The brother/sister dynamic is as old as the story of Cain and Abel. Sibling rivalries are normal in life even though they aren't excusable. Young people would like to deal with these problems with their brothers and sisters, but they don't always know how to.

Some of the specific concerns that surface between siblings are of parental origination. I mean mom and dad create the problems! Kids write about conspicuous parental favoritism. They resent unfavorable comparing of brothers and sisters as a means of motivating to greater achievement. They believe all that does is drive a wedge between them and someone they would like to like. They are turned off by uneven and inconsistent expectations.

Grandmas get into the picture too. Grandmother has usually moved in after granddad has died. True? Now, in new surroundings, while dealing with the death of her long-term companion, she finds herself alone, somewhat shocked, yearning for recognition and desiring social relationships. In order to gain those things, she often finds herself in the position of competing for attention with her teenage grandchild. When the teenager discovers that grandma is a rival, all kinds of strange things can happen. Some tense and difficult moments can develop. They ought to find in each other a loving source of help and reinforcement, but instead they become antagonists.

Parents need to realize the difficulty between grandma and grandchild and become "brokers" when tension develops between the two. Grandmother needs to have her moment. That can't be denied. But her teenage grandchild needs prime time too. So there's another good reason for having parents. You need to make sure that grandmother and grandchild stay friends!

Number four—friends

The fourth area of teenage concern revolves around other boys and girls. It took me a long time to understand that most teenagers accent the second word: boy *friends* and girl *friends*. They yearn for friends of the opposite sex. Friends, together, can discover what it means to be who they are and how better to understand those who are not like them.

That's not to suggest that there are no sexual aspects to the attraction between boys and girls. There are. But I want to accent that the primary driving and significant need teenagers have *is not sexual*. It's social. Their curiosity about each other is much more complicated than a preoccupation with procreation. In wanting to know others, they are yearning to discover what it means to be persons. They believe the best way to discover personness in themselves is to discover the personness in someone else. They are right.

Would you be surprised if I told you the question most often asked by seventh and eighth grade boys is, "How do I ask a girl to dance?" They aren't asking for directions. The thrust of that question is discovering how to deal with rejection. The clearer question would be, "What do you do when you ask a girl to dance and she declines?" Boys at that age are beginning to learn that pushing, shoving, and pulling hair are not the best approach to the opposite sex. But they're not sure what is better.

A later teenage question, again most often asked by the young man, is, "How do you talk with a girl?" This question is an early recognition that conversation is an important part of living. The sad part is they don't have much help from anyone in learning how to talk.

As I reflect on 30 years of dealing with teenage premarital pregnancy, I think almost all the young women who come to mind have some common characteristics. (And when I knew who the hidden father was, the characteristics seemed to fit him too.) They had low self-esteem, hesitancy in speech, uncertainty of body language, difficulty verbalizing, and minimal social skills. I suggest to parents that an excellent way to help their son or daughter face sexual temptation is to teach them how to talk. I'm convinced that many premarital pregnancies originate with a fine young man and woman in the back seat of a car who get sexually stimulated because they don't know how to be conversationally stimulating.

I don't believe classes in conversation are going to guarantee moral propriety! But I believe they will help. Let's teach our teens how to talk. What do we have to lose? More important, what do they have to gain?

Number five—you'll never believe it

I didn't believe it. When the facts surfaced, I found it difficult to accept that teens wanted a closer relationship to their church and that they had a yen to know their pastor better.

Supporting evidence for this discovery is in *A Study of Generations* (Augsburg, 1970), a book based on one of the most thorough investigations of any denomination ever made. Other studies substantiate the conclusion that teenagers are much more spiritual, and much more inclined toward church life, than many had previously assumed.

One of the conclusions of *A Study of Generations*, based on extensive interviews, was that there is a low-water mark of belief among Lutherans. Belief bottoms out, on the average, at the 22nd year. The slippage starts at 15, a kind of belief peak. My mail suggests this slippage is usually preceded by an effort of young people to get closer to their church and their pastor. I'll expand more on that in a later chapter, but for the moment it's exciting to realize how intensively spiritual young people actually are. It's also important for all of us to realize how turned off they can become by the failure of the church, or the clergy, to live up to the spiritual and moral expectations that church and clergy have taught the young! Not only were teenagers taught these things, they believed them. May God have mercy on those who steal the spiritual confidence of the young!

Wrap-up: deal direct!

What else do teenagers write me about? Everything! There are questions about drugs, very specific inquiries about sex, many concerns about vocational problems, apprehensions on a wide variety of other subjects. They care about cars, stepbrothers, world economics, money, their rights. It goes on and on and on. In summary, they care about all types of real-life concerns.

You could sleuth out what's happening yourself, if you want to. But let me warn you—sudden direct parental questioning after years of conversational neglect generally doesn't get much more than a shrug at first. But keep it up. Keep talking to your kids. Correct past neglect a little bit at a time. Do some careful observing. Improve your listening skills. You'll be surprised—and better informed.

One remaining emphasis: don't be afraid to deal directly with your teenagers. They like it. That's a fact.

If they act like children (I mean *really act like children*), then treat them as children. Do it without "put-down" language. Later in life, when they put away childish things (as St. Paul suggests in 1 Corinthians 13), happily meet them at their new and improved level. If you're not quite sure whether they're acting like children or adults, ask them. If you're confused by the messages they send, request interpretations. Those elementary approaches to your son or daughter are available to you—if you're not afraid.

The teen years are gone—quickly. Whatever we develop with our children during those years will be the building blocks from which later relationships are constructed. Put down a solid foundation. We live with our mistakes, or our blessings, for a long time.

I receive many letters from pastors and professional youth workers who want help with teenagers. When the letters come, the writers generally describe the young people they work with in the worst of terms, using the least attractive teenage moments as illustrations. I write back. Somewhere toward the end of the letter I try to put together a series of sentences like this: "What's really upsetting you, my friend, is that these kids are just being kids. You may think of them as adults, but remember, they are *young* adults."

Being a teenager means that in many circumstances you don't use the best judgment and you aren't always fully aware of the consequences of your actions. Teenagers make mistakes and pay for them. They will profit by experience and learn to make more considered decisions with the passing of time. When that takes place, we change their name. Teenagers who are in full control of themselves, who have a clear set of specific objectives, who sense the needs of others, and who handle themselves with mature dependability in every circumstance have a special name. We call them adults. Grown-ups. *You can help them become what you would like them to be if you will start by accepting them as they are right now.*

Study teenagers as they are. In knowing them, you'll learn a lot more about yourself. Whether you clearly recall it or not, you went through the very same stages. Yes, you did! The kind of person you are today is rooted in those teen years.

Now, there's one more important source of fundamental information we must explore if we are to be able to say with joy, "Thank God I have a teenager." That source of fundamental information is Scripture itself.

I am confident that you'll be surprised by what the Bible says about teenagers and how the biblical approach to them strengthens you and gives you a helping hand that really helps. We'll move on in that direction now. Ready?

5 The Bible's View of Teens— Believe It

The Bible? Does the Bible specifically talk about teenagers? I'll give you the answer in one word: no. The Bible says nothing specific about *teenagers* or the significant years from 12 to 20. Don't misunderstand me. There are a lot of teenagers in the Bible, and the teen years are obviously important to the Bible writers. As a matter of fact, the only story in Scripture about Jesus in the period between his birth and when he began his public ministry at about 30 is one that took place at the very edge of his teens—when he was 12. Even so, the Bible doesn't say anything about teenagers or deal with teenagers *as a special age category* as we do. Maybe, after we hear what Scripture has to say, we won't talk about teenagers in the same way any more either.

Setting the stage

Before we study the Bible's view, let's make sure we agree on how most people today see teenagers. For most people the teen years are one of life's chronological stages, right? First you are a child. Then you are a teenager. Then you are an adult. Then you are an old man or woman. Each of those stages is distinct and separate. It's a matter of going from step to step to step to step—one, two, three, four.

Do you agree that for most people there is a boundary line between being a child and being a teenager; between being a teenager and adult; between being an adult and being an old person? And, if we're going to complete the sequence, isn't the very last step death, and the first, birth? Don't most people believe that the sequence of life goes like this: birth, childhood, teenage, adult, old age, death? Six steps. Six steps from the beginning to the end—from start to finish—with teenage as one of the steps.

If you believe that there is a six-step sequence to life, you are in for a surprise. You can't find those six steps in the Bible. The best you will do is four: birth, childhood, adult, death. Cradle to grave. Maybe there's a fifth distinct step, if you twist scriptural view around enough, but that fifth step isn't the teenage category. It's old age. What is omitted entirely? The teens.

There is no biblical talk about the teens as a separate and distinct stage. In the Bible, people moved from being children to being adults with no interim pause. The end of being a child was around age 12, and being an adult started from the same point. At 12 or early 13, you were a *young adult*, but an *adult* nonetheless.

Think with me for a few moments about the young people you know in the Bible. There was a young—very young— Samuel. He was clearly a child, but God sent an adult message for others through him.

How about the Bible's treatment of Joseph? Sold in slavery at 17, he entered upon a venture that peaked when he was 30 as second in command of all Egypt! But it started at 17. Moses, Daniel, Shadrach, Meshach, Abednego, David—they all started their pilgrimages as active participants in life's drama (not just as onlookers) at young and tender ages.

These examples are consistent with the entirety of the Old Testament attitude toward the young—even children. They must be involved in the whole of what's going on (Josh. 8:35, for example) and must be brought along on all the adventures (Exod. 10:8-11). That theme continues with Jesus' insistence that little children be brought to him and not be held back (Matt. 19:13-15). For an eye-opener, read through the whole of Scripture, with all your senses attuned, looking for how God treats and involves the children and the young adults. He treats them with dignity. He has high expectations. He deals with them as we deal with few adults!

In the 20th century it's different. We don't include; we exclude. Children (and teenagers too) are "spared" most of life's real moments; from the very things in which Scripture specifically involves them, we isolate, insulate, and shelter them. Scripture seeks participation and looks for commitment from the young. Scripture calls them part of the family, treats them as young adults, makes them responsible individuals. But not most of us.

There *are* segments of our society that treat teenagers differently than do most Christians. The military, for example. I sometimes wonder how many 15- or 16- or 17-year-old young men and women went into battle and died heroically serving their country. Were they too young? Too young to die? In the military, young men and women are given the same treatment and opportunities for failure or success that their older companions in arms receive.

Another cultural segment that sees teenagers differently is the street gangs and the jail/prison populous. In those surroundings, anyone who is old enough to commit an adult crime is old enough to be dealt with as an adult. The cruel initiations that young people experience in prisons and in gangs offend all but the worst in our society. But demanding adult responses from those we call "kids" is part of that world.

It's strange. God, gangs, generals, and jails (what an odd mingling) all have something in common when it comes to teens: they treat them as adults. I won't say much more about generals, jails, or gangs, but I surely want to say more about God. Let's look at the evidences of his attitude.

One of the clearest pictures we have of God's attitude toward young people is one we have already talked about (in Chapter 3): the cutting of the umbilical cord in the human birthing process. As soon as babies come into this very different world, they are on their own. Oh, yes, God surrounds babies with support systems of parents and other protections. But the real drama is lived out *by the infants* as, from the moment of birth, they begin the process of absolutely essential, but fully independent, responses.

The point? One of the larger problems of making it through the teens is that some of us older folks seem to think sons and daughters are still connected to us with a kind of umbilical cord. We try to attach them to our ideas and thoughts and views and desires, making them dependent on us.

But that's not the approach God demonstrates. While God does seek to influence life, he lays aside all coercive directing. It is possible to do it the way we want, says God. While God accents parental protection, support, and encouragement, *we* tilt toward force, manipulation, and control. Isn't it marvelous that God's sun and rain come to all those who need it (Matt. 5:45), whether they are good or not? God keeps a promise of even-handed interest and support without insisting that every one of life's decisions must be directed by him. God suggests, encourages, and carefully watches but does not dominate, manipulate, or regally control.

Against that background, I reflect upon the thousands of letters I receive from teens. They talk about misplaced and heavy-handed parental "helpfulness." How different with the Lord! While he doesn't turn us loose on life with nary a care about right and wrong, he also doesn't smother us with repressive directions or tug us around as if we were puppies on leashes.

Our hardheartedness and resolute ignorance bring much

pain into life, for sure. But even when we're sinning, the Lord does not force his way upon us. Advice? Yes! Force? No. He treats us as older than we are and better than we deserve. In so doing, he "hints" at a better way for us to deal with others, teenagers included.

Does the Lord deal with children differently than with adults? Somewhat, but not as differently as we might at first think. The major difference is that he supports children with a unique gift: parents who are responsible for them and supportive families to help them in their earliest years. He puts children in families under parental protection and direction. However, once the boundary of childhood is passed, full parental/family responsibility is terminated. It is replaced by individual responsibility and self-control.

During the opening dozen years of life, the family has a significant and divinely ordained direct responsibility. How parents exert that responsibility, and how well they exert it, has a lasting effect for life. But after those early years pass, the relationship is different. *Adult* teenagers must claim increasing responsibility for their actions. At the same time, the role of parents shifts too. Maybe that's the most important message we can receive from the one Bible story of Jesus' early life.

Jesus' adventure at 12

As a parent, I often confuse the importance of doing something correctly with the necessity of teaching a young person how to do something independently. I mix up achieving with learning how to achieve. It's most difficult to see my child of 13 or 15 as an adult.

Mary had that problem. Joseph had that problem. They had difficulty seeing Jesus as an adult. Let's read about it.

> Every year the parents of Jesus went to Jerusalem for the Passover Festival. When Jesus was twelve years old, they went to the festival as usual. When the festival was over, they started back home, but the boy Jesus stayed in Jerusalem. His

parents did not know this; they thought that he was with the group, so they traveled a whole day and then started looking for him among their relatives and friends. They did not find him, so they went back to Jerusalem looking for him. On the third day they found him in the Temple, sitting with the Jewish teachers, listening to them and asking questions. All who heard him were amazed at his intelligent answers. His parents were astonished when they saw him, and his mother said to him, "Son, why have you done this to us? Your father and I have been terribly worried trying to find you."

He answered them, "Why did you have to look for me? Didn't you know that I had to be in my Father's house?" But they did not understand his answer.

So Jesus went back with them to Nazareth, where he was obedient to them. His mother treasured all these things in her heart. Jesus grew both in body and in wisdom, gaining favor with God and men.

Luke 2:41-52

This story reads differently if you recognize that the trip to Jerusalem was the beginning of Jesus' adult life. At 12, he was a man. That's why they took him along. Many Jews today recognize the experience Jesus underwent as the equivalent of a *bar mitzvah*. A *bar mitzvah* is a ceremony that, among other things, marks the beginning of recognized manhood. With that in mind, listen again to Mary's angry/glad/joyous/upset/relieved/mother's greeting: "Your father and I have been looking for you everywhere!"

Any teenager in the world knows that when a mother starts the sentence with "Your father and I," there is trouble afoot. That's a heavy opening. It's ominous. Sparks will surely fly.

And sparks flew. He didn't duck his head and humbly mutter, "I'm sorry." He didn't offer a limp explanation like "I forgot what time it was" or "Wasn't I supposed to meet you here?" He talked right back to Mary. He spoke up to her like a grown-up. In quick succession he made two adult points.

One point was that he had a responsibility superior to a mother's concern. The Father's business needed attention. Like it or not, it was his priority.

Second, he showed surprise that Mary would not immediately know where he was. Why did it take her three days to find him in the only place for Jesus: his Father's house?

Those are strong words from a teenager. Those are tough words to a mother. Notwithstanding, that's what Jesus said to Mary and what Mary had to learn to live with—all because Jesus was an adult.

When I first heard those words as a boy in Kansas, I figured the reason Jesus got away with his remark was that he was the Son of God. If I had talked to my mom that way, I would have been in great difficulty.

But I was wrong. Jesus was not being an impertinent young snip, pushing his mom around. He was making a significant theological point, one as appropriate today as then: teenagers are adults who are obligated before God for responsible adult service. Mary and Joseph had done the right thing in bringing Jesus to Jerusalem as a sign of his coming of age. Now Jesus was doing the right thing by acting his age. From a mother's viewpoint, Jesus showed incredibly bad judgment and cruel insensitivity to parental apprehension. From Jesus' own perspective, he was acting the way that all grown-up sons of God ought.

20th-century congregations and 12-year-olds

Most congregations treat their teens the way Mary treated Jesus. They have low and limited expectations of them. While many congregations confirm their kids at 12 or 13— or put them through some other kind of coming-of-age ceremony—they often do so without seriousness or studied purpose. It is a rite, a ritual, a ceremony. Nothing is really changed. Little is expected. A big splashy moment, packed with all kinds of liturgical drama and a public exacting of awesome promises from young people; then back to normal. Many assume the kids aren't taking it very seriously, and many kids know that the parents aren't taking it seriously. Do you believe this paragraph? Test it.

What is the first "adult" decision teenagers face after they've gone through their confirmation or whatever-else experience? Isn't it whether they will keep going to Sunday school and Bible class like they used to, or whether they can now parrot their parents and stay home? That's about all the "spiritual struggle" they face. You try to name something else teens are expected to do—an adult thing—in the church. And if you name one, name two!

I have a plea. I have a plea on behalf of teenagers—and from the will of God. If we're going to insinuate that teens are adults through confirmation, then let's treat them as adults. Let's expect exactly the same thing from them that we expect from other active adult Christians. Let's give them the same opportunities for service and leadership and responsibility as we give to others—and urge that they claim them. Let them vote. Allow them to hold any office in the church. Urge them to participate in everything, *limited only by their abilities, not their age.*

The church is not a private club with some members having rights and responsibilities that others do not. It is the body of Christ (1 Cor. 12:27). The only restrictions on any part of the body are the restrictions that God places on all parts. Limit a teenager's role by capability, never by birthdays!

The continuing need and history of teenage deeds must be honored. Anything proper that they can accomplish must be permitted. We must stir up and encourage their active participation. Little David, rather than anyone else in Israel, fought Goliath for the simplest reason: he was the best available choice on the scene—and the only volunteer. Many a worldly Goliath is still stalking around, untamed and undestroyed, because we have told our Davids (and Davidas) they are too young. We are wrong!

But let's get back to our Bible story. There are two other significant lessons to be learned from Luke 2.

More lessons from Luke

First, Jesus returned with his parents to Nazareth and placed himself under their authority (Luke 2:51). That needs to be noted. While claiming the appropriate adult role, Jesus did not act as if he had nothing more to learn from mom and dad. He just had nothing more to learn from them *as a child*.

I would assume that Mary never again spoke to Jesus in quite the same way she did in that electric moment in the Temple. Her changed approach freed him to be the kind of obedient and helpful son that God wants in all families. Honoring parents is a life-long responsibility and a great Christian pleasure. It is the duty of a child and the privilege of an adult.

Christ's example also instructs teenagers, and parents, that important roles remain for moms and dads during the teen-age adult years. Those roles are not the same as they were a generation ago, but there still is a significant aspect of teacher/learner in the parent/teenager relationship. Parents are teachers and teenagers learners—most of the time. No one pops across the boundary of childhood into the earliest adult years as a completed product. A lot of finishing work needs to be done. We have much to learn with and from each other.

Another lesson from Luke is that, having settled his parental relationship, Jesus was ready to get on about the basic task of the teen years—*growing*. The King James Version of the Bible describes that process beautifully in this way: "And Jesus increased in wisdom and stature, and in favor with God and man" (Luke 2:52).

You must understand the word *increase*. It means more

than that Jesus grew larger. The root meaning of that Greek word refers to hacking your way through tangled growth. It's as if the teen years are a dense jungle that must be penetrated, machete in hand. That sounds accurate to me!

The word also means to "beat into shape," as if pounding red-hot metal on a blacksmith's anvil, working to force a new form on the raw, shapeless metal. *Increase*, appropriately and properly defined, has the feel of the teenage years. Don't you agree?

That one sentence in Scripture captures the drama of those incredible early adult years while at the same time putting a finger on teenagers' most important task: growing. That task breaks down into four distinct areas of activity. Let's talk about them one by one.

God wants you to get smart

We'll start at the beginning of the biblical list. Growing means getting wiser. That tells us that God expects us to get smarter. We are to keep on learning both practical and theoretical things through the entirety of life, but God certainly expects us to be about that task in the teen years.

Successful lives require sharpened intellectual abilities. There are few free rides in life. Those that look like they might be free may start out that way, but they usually end up to be incredibly high priced. Kids need to know that. One of the most important parental responsibilities is helping young people understand that wisdom is crucial to life. It must be developed.

Wisdom includes all kinds of things: vocational skills, academic excellence, occupational experiences, factual data, logical accomplishments, and anything else that falls within the broad boundaries of what we call "schooling." The biblical principle is that everyone needs to increase in wisdom. There can be no truants in life—no educational drop-outs, no intellectual goof-offs. Whether the schooling is formal or informal, the *increasing* process demands that we develop all the smarts that we can.

But what if the wisdom my son wants is not the wisdom I want him to have? Or, to be more specific, what if I think my daughter ought to be a computer specialist and she seems determined on horse care? By whatever the process, our parental responsibility is to help young people determine and develop the skills that *they* have. We are to help them make *their* choices. Those choices may or may not be the ones that we have in mind. If there comes a conflict between your choice and their choices, their choices will win ultimately. The best you can do is help them understand that your choice might be more appropriate and lead them to claim it as their own. How?

There are plenty of places to test young people. There are organizations that give very direct hints about appropriate careers. There are people who specialize in career guidance. Parents who have been building a relationship of trust across the years can cash in at these moments with a gusto! They can directly suggest to their son or daughter specific courses of action and follow them through—together.

This, regrettably, is also the time when many parents discover they haven't built relationships. They discover that their sons and daughters see them only as a source of constant criticism and discouragement, not help. If, for any reason, you find yourself in that fix, what do you do then?

Errant parents (whether the title is deserved or not) can do what Scripture tells us all. Admit mistakes as you see them, or as they are pointed out to you, and ask for forgiveness. Parents who discover they have messed things up, consciously or unconsciously, need to know that the best thing to do is own up to the mistake and plead for understanding and forgiveness.

If things are so confused that you can't talk to your sons or daughters, help them find assistance from someone else who has been meaningful in their lives. Encourage them toward someone they trust. A teacher? Another parent in the neighborhood? A grandparent?

Never forget that you are not alone. God did not give parental responsibility to two people without supplying other kinds of support. There are lots of folks around, many within our homes, who will help us when we are right and who will also help us when we are wrong. It's only when we decide to bluster our way through and force our will that things really don't work out well.

So help your teenager come to an understanding of the importance of wisdom—and how best to attain it. OK?

It's a physical thing too

Our next teenage task for teens, as taught by Luke, is "increase in stature."

Do you know what that means? I bet you've said many times, "That boy is growing like a weed. I hardly get him home from the store with a pair of pants and the legs are already an inch too short." Or, "She's turned into a woman practically overnight. Yesterday she was my little girl, and today she's a grown woman. Looks like her mom."

Growing up physically is a significant and continuing teenage task. While much of the process is automatic, it still requires supportive parental presence in several areas. One of those areas is providing food.

Growing up demands lots of food—nutritional food. That's where parents come in. Parents are the ones who can supply and encourage and provide guidance toward the best foods.

Physical growing also means confronting exciting bodily changes while needing almost unbelievable amounts of sleep. Not all the sleeping teenagers do is laziness. By no means. Their physical needs are not the same as those of us who are older, and they should not be judged on our basis. The physical aspects of growing are physically draining. Lots of calories and lots of rest are needed.

Exercise also is a part of the physical growing-up process. What some used to call "horsing around" was actually much more serious. We were developing endurance and building strength while testing ourselves for physical agility. All of that is important to the teenage experience.

We also need to remember that there are physical experiences that don't help. Drugs, marijuana, and alcohol are not for experimentation at any age and certainly not at a time in life when they can do so much damage to a young body. Be sure your teens know that, but not through nagging—through knowledge.

Irresponsible driving or foolish risk taking are other physical experiences that need to be bypassed. All those are areas where teens need help from parents. But how do you give it?

The surest way to give help to teenagers is to practice in your life the things you want them to implement in theirs. Teach them the better things to do, physically, by doing those better things yourself. *Show* them how to take care of their bodies.

Make sure they understand that the warnings offered to them at school, and through their physical counselors, are important. Never laugh or joke about serious instruction. Learn for yourself what those warnings are, and how dangerous physical abuses are to your son or daughter. That's one reason we ought to stay active in P.T.A., even at the high school level. Programs offering crucial information for parents are regularly presented by others equally concerned and better informed. Your presence is a witness to your son or daughter of how seriously you take their well-being.

Simply put, make it your business to know and understand your teenager's physical needs. Then help them to take care of themselves.

The love for God

The third task for teens from Luke? Developing "favor with God."

"Favor with God" covers so much. It includes spiritual growth, a developing devotional life, sustained activities in worship, participation in service before God. Spiritual growth happens in and through all of those things.

It's a wise congregation (with wise parents in membership) that actively seeks to involve its young people in worship and in other significant expressions of church life—not just as audience but as actors. Young people need experiences that are much more spiritual than an occasional opportunity to put on a play or run a Saturday car wash!

Everything in the worship world should be open to them. Everything possible should be done to draw them into involvement. Instead of an occasional Teen Sunday, make every Sunday a Teen Sunday. Give them regular visibility as ushers, lectors, speakers, teachers, musicians, and participants in the parish Sunday celebration, limited only by their ability and spiritual commitment.

Of course, there will be special moments and necessary times of separateness. But one of the most intense requirements of the teenage years is experiencing spiritual unity with parents. There needs to be a regular chance for teenagers to practice their faith side by side with mom or dad. My correspondence with teenagers underlines that they want to be part of the local congregation. Sad to say, local congregations are not always conscious of this desire, nor are they willing to make adequate provisions. Only when a local congregation is faced with survival does it become interested in its young people. Then it's often too late. The best way to keep young people in the church is to never put them out or set them aside or ignore them.

Encourage a personal devotional life too. Talk about and practice prayer. Encourage home and personal Bible study. The teen years are a great time for developing interest in all these areas.

And don't forget the great spiritual moments that take place at various camps and gatherings. Teen trips, worship around a campfire, common experiences with other young people—all "feed" the faith.

Learning to like and to be liked

I've had a little something to do with a number of super-sized youth gatherings. I call 10,000 or more in one place a super-sized gathering. In one sense that gathering itself really doesn't do much for the kids. (Before you flip to the next paragraph, be sure you finish this one in its totality. I don't want you to misunderstand me.) I believe the *greatest* benefit of those super-sized gatherings is not the gathering but the *trip to the gathering*. In planning to go to the gathering, and then in the trip itself, teenagers learn how to work together, raise money together, take a long trip together, and share significant experiences together.

It would be absolutely OK with me if the 10,000 kids who were coming to the super-sized event would journey to any given point in the United States, enter a large stadium, look around for a moment to see what 10,000 Christian kids in one place look like, and then get back in the buses or vans and head for home. The going and the coming, plus the sight of so many other young people, is the powerful medicine of the moment, in my estimation. Traveling and planning and sharing are all part of learning how to increase "in favor with man," Luke's fourth task. Learning how to deal with people as you embark on a common project and learning how to be a social creature are primary learning tasks of the teen years. Socializing is not just fun; socializing is necessary.

There is another great socializing benefit in those trips to youth gatherings. For many youngsters, this is their first time around adults *other than their parents*. There are lots of adults at youth gatherings. Some are counselors. Some are musicians. Some are teachers, chaplains, speakers. There are adult helpers of all kinds.

Kids go looking for adults at gatherings. I'm happy to report that adults go looking for kids as well. These adults are not trying to recapture their lost youth. Most would actually rather be home with their own families. But they realize that they are helping teens through a social growth experience—an experience that can only take place in an environment different from home. Social growth is a remarkably important aspect of the teen experience. Jesus dealt with it; so does every other young person in the world. It will be a good or bad experience, depending on how it's treated, but it will certainly be an experience.

So much for the four tasks. My comments don't exhaust the subjects, but I do hope they alert parents to the importance of each. There yet remains one more significant thing to say about the four. Simply put, *one dare never assume that any one of the four tasks is more important than any other.* All are of equal significance. All are necessary growing tasks. Experiencing three out of four is not acceptable. It must be four-for-four.

When teens have struggled and toughened their way through the challenge of intellectual, physical, spiritual, and social growth, genuine maturity takes place. That's what the Bible is trying to teach us. If you don't believe the Bible on its own merits, then you ought to know that everything in life, and all the life sciences, would agree with that last evaluative sentence. Persons dwarfed or stunted in any of the four areas will have much difficulty in the postteen years and will never be the people they could have been.

Three more points

There are still three points I need to present in this chapter. Each is important. Each is direct. Each is scriptural.

1. Not every teenager will respond to every growth opportunity in the same way. Another way of saying this is that there are Marys and there are Marthas. There are young people who are less inclined to large groups and there are those who are strongly drawn to massive gatherings. But don't worry. God never intended that all teens be alike. As long as no extremes are being experienced, the growth process can happen. The speed of growth, however, is related to the individual. It doesn't happen as quickly for one as for another. Movement is more important in the growing process than the speed of movement.

2. Once you're beyond minimum requirements, there will be different levels of excellence in all four categories of growth. Translated, this means that some teens will be more physical than others; some more intellectual; some more spiritual; some more social. *All* must pass the basic training. After that, the unique aspects of the individual character take over. The Bible is filled with different kinds of people.

3. The task of growing is impossible alone. I don't just mean that there needs to be other human beings around to support teens during this period. I also mean that God gives direct assistance. He hears and he answers prayers. He gives strength to accomplish with him what could never be accomplished without him.

And one last thought for you, as a parent. God is not only the God of your sons and daughters. He's not only the God of teens. He's the God of mothers and fathers. He not only watches over the young and the weak, but the old and wise as well. His interest is not only toward those who are simple, but toward those who are simply frustrated. Turn to him in prayer and in faith. Ask the Father, in Jesus' name, to make you the kind of person you want to be. He will guide you toward being a better parent, a finer individual, a more helpful spouse.

This chapter needs reflecting upon. It's not brush-over-quickly information. If mother Mary could "treasure all these things in her heart," so can the rest of us. It's only when you really understand what a teenager is that you can begin to say with joy, "Thank God I have a teenager."

Now let's get on to some special concerns and the development of special parental and family skills.

6 Family First Aid

From time to time I make myself stop and reflect upon the kind of teenager I'm dealing with and writing about. The teenagers I deal with are just average—no extremes. Extremes (super good or super bad) call for distinct and specialized consideration. I'm glad there are those who deal with the kids on the extreme ends of the spectrum. I deal with the great middle. I have chosen to.

Don't think for a moment that the great middle has no needs. One of the greatest needs the middle has is attention and care. Because they look so healthy, and because they seem to get through most situations with minimal attention, the kids in the great middle of the teenage world are basically left alone, abandoned to their low-level problems. Most kids make it by themselves, so leave them alone—that's a common philosophy.

But we can't leave them alone. We don't want to risk scarring and crippling difficulties in the transition from childhood to recognition as a full-fledged adult. In addition, even though they could make it through alone, we parents want to be involved and know, for ourselves, that everything is OK.

This chapter is for parents *and* teenagers. In fact, it is for entire families. It contains family living "medicines," the equivalent of your home first-aid kit's bandages, aspirin, and disinfectants. Having those supplies around, ready for inevitable use, assures you that most of the little injuries of normal living will not become serious.

But this chapter is more than that. It is precrisis stuff. It is preventative. Properly utilized it will guarantee as much family and teenager health as it is possible to have. It will help keep all of you at the peak of vigor and unity.

The specifics we're going to talk about are family *communication*, effective family *problem solving*, and family *modeling*. Let's talk about those helpful preventative and/or healing agents one at a time.

Family communication—watch your words

I keep two rhymes about communication in mind at all times. The first reads like this:

> Before man first learned to write to be read,
> There was endless dispute as to what a man said.
> Now that we write, it's plain to be seen,
> There is endless dispute as to what our words mean.

That verse contains many messages. One of the most significant is that words are slippery little rascals. They can bless and build. They can also confuse and confound. Agree?

Now to my second rhyme:

> The words I speak are soft and sweet—
> I never know which ones I'll eat.

The unspoken word is often the most helpful and generally the least dangerous.

With those two rhymes in mind, I'd like to surface some obvious things about communication. Most of them you already know but keep forgetting. Let's start with this: *words have power.*

Words are not neutral. Even innocuous small talk contains a potent message. Casual conversation communicates casual concern. That may not be the message you intended to send, or at least not the message you thought you intended. But that's the message that came through.

Words have power. When you start hooking them together, a tremendous force builds. Whether they are used for conscious persuading or intentional condemning or careless criticizing or intentional loving, words have an energy all their own. "I love you." "You little baby, you!" "How dumb can you get?" "You can do it!" Look at the power for good—or evil—in those four phrases!

However, *words aren't our only means of communication*. Signs, even nonverbal signs, communicate. Facial expressions communicate. Actions communicate. Silence communicates. Communication is a wide-ranging and complex process by which you move a message from your heart and mind into the heart and mind of someone else, by whatever means. You could be sending two messages simultaneously—one verbal, one nonverbal. What if they conflict?

Another important insight is that *it takes at least two to communicate*. A writer and a reader must work together if a book is to be useful. Both the speaker and the hearer struggle with a point; one to explain, the other to understand. Unless both sender and receiver are working at the communication process, the message is often garbled, or incomplete, or confusing, or (worst of all) susceptible to multiple interpretations. Applying those negative potentials to your family's communication makes it clear that both parent and teenager must be constantly and actively involved in building good communication processes in the home.

Doing what comes unnaturally

If communication isn't going on very well at home, what can you do about it? Are there ways to make the communication task more dependable? The answer is yes! The most obvious way to claim that answer is by taking a course in communication.

A course in communication? You mean we could go to school to learn how to talk? Why would anyone want to take a course in doing something that is already so natural?

Communication isn't natural. It's not a gift that some automatically possess. It's a *learned* skill that all ought, but only some do, develop. If you believe that people can be taught to drive a car, or sew a dress, or bake a turkey, then it's at least reasonable that people can be taught to talk and hear. And where better to learn than in a school?

There are easily accessible "schools" of communication all around us. I doubt if anyone is more than a few minutes away from a church, or an educational institution, or a local association that is teaching communication skills. Look around. One of the most useful processes for learning and improving communication that I've come upon is called Parent Effectiveness Training (P.E.T.).

P.E.T. is the brainchild of Dr. Thomas Gordon. From him I learned all kinds of interesting communication skills, not the least of which is something he calls *active listening*. He believes that listening is a skill that can be learned or improved through training. Real hearing is more than a passive attentiveness with which some may or may not be born. He believes that listening can be taught. I certainly agree.

But a warning must be issued about active listening. What sometimes happens is that as the parent/teenager communication process improves, there seems to be an intensification, not a diminishing, of family friction.

Why? The answer is really quite simple.

As communication gets better, family members, for the first time, really hear what the other person is saying. That may not always make them feel good. They may not like what is finally being clearly communicated. Had they been listening better across the years, they would have already heard (and probably resolved) what they now don't like hearing. But their previous inadequate listening skills shielded them from the truth the other person had been saying for quite some time.

That's only one side of developing communication skills—the bad side. The good side is that as you develop better hearing, it helps you not only hear the criticisms but also the loving and caring things as well. In any case, hearing the truth is your only real hope for ultimately solving a problem and getting on to finer things.

Keep this clear: communication doesn't make the problems; communication exposes problems that have always existed. But it also can expose the way to possible improvement. Good communication is like walking through dense underbrush on a dark night with a beaming flashlight in hand. The light doesn't make the tangles in the shrubbery. It only exposes them. With the light you travel more quickly and securely as its bright finger exposes potential areas of difficulty.

Communication dangers

In family communication, there are a number of things we all need to be warned about. High on my list is an urgent warning to *avoid pejorative terms*. A pejorative term is a put-down word: *dumb, young, stupid, childish, selfish*. Those words (and so many others), even when accurately applied, don't build. They destroy. They clog the hearing process.

So why do we use them? They're usually intended to pressure and force, to intimidate and demean. They are like clubs or whips or pointed pistols. They are intended to pressure others to do things that you want done, at any cost. The cost is invariably too high. Look out for pejorative and demeaning words.

A second communication caution is this: *avoid you-messages*. A you-message is a message that dumps on the other person. Here's an example: "There you go again. You really know how to make me mad. You sit there at the table without a napkin and you get me upset. You got me so upset that my spoon fell in the soup and spotted the tablecloth. It's all your fault." That's a you-message. It forces blame on someone else.

Instead, use I-messages. Compare the above message with an I-message. The speaker might have said: "I wish I could change, Fred, but I suppose I never will. From the time I was a little girl, my mother drummed into me the need to use napkins at the table. She told me it was the first mark of manners. I don't know whether that's true, and I'm not sure that other people feel as I do today, but I can't shake off my training. I would appreciate it if you would help me be more comfortable when we eat together by using your napkin."

I don't know if Fred will obey or whether he will say, "Oh, mommmm!!", but I do know that he won't end up storming away from the table or that all of you won't finish your supper in angry silence, eating with clenched jaws and smoldering eyes. Over the long pull, an I-message is a thousand times more effective as a means of teaching and communication than a you-message. I-messages build. They make for peace and tranquility in a home. They control pejorative words and accent speaking with a kind of clarity and a nonjudgmental tenderness that make it easier for other people to hear.

Communication involves two people, *but each is doing an important and different thing*. That's the third warning flag I want to wave. Senders need to search for the best "language" they can find, whether in words written or words spoken or by nonverbal signs. (We've already talked about that.) *Receivers need to consciously eliminate distractions that can mix up the sender's message*. Receivers need to achieve and maintain eye contact with the speaker and offer their concentrated attention. The receiver's face is one of the most important clues the sender can study to discover whether the message is received. A smile, a frown, a grimace—all hint at what has been heard.

But there are more cautions than that! Do you realize that we sometimes *intentionally* send ambiguous or conflicting messages? An ambiguous or conflicting message is when our face says one thing and our words say another. Or when we say, "Maybe." An ambiguous or conflicting message guarantees a kind of victory for the sender. No matter how things work out, he can either say, "That's what I meant from the beginning," or, "You didn't understand me." Victories under those circumstances are high priced—*too* high priced. They may help you feel successful, but they destroy family unity, and they never bring a blessing.

Everyone in the family must understand the basic components of communication. Determine to be a better sender and an improved receiver. If the family (or you) begins with that resolution, the situation at home will quickly improve. Once the family members start moving in the right direction, they won't stop. Why should they? Things are only getting better, and who doesn't like that?

So be sure to place into your family first-aid kit a family-sized tube of effective communication. If you don't have one there already, get one as quickly as you can. It helps healing and prevents family friction. All it requires is some time and energy.

Problem solving in the home

Let's suppose that through your efforts communication improves. Let's suppose that you and your son or daughter understand what each other is saying with increased clarity. Now what? It may seem to you that through better communication you have blundered into new areas of tension and differences so rugged and wild that there appears to be no way of resolving them. Hearing one another clearly will also mean hearing one another's differences clearly. If all we're going to get is more tension, what's the value of improved communication?

Improved communication is not an end in itself. It is a means to a very important end: family unity. Improved communication can never stand alone. Communication skills don't resolve differences. They only set the stage for something else: the possibility of confronting and resolving family differences. I call it problem solving.

You should have been with me in New Orleans one Saturday when a hundred or so teenagers and the same number of parents were gathered to do a job of communicating. And were they ever doing it! They had focused their attention on a single concern—*clean rooms.*

They were doing a great job of communicating, but what they weren't doing was a great job of problem solving. Parents and kids were talking back and forth, clearly, for about an hour. They were using good words, helpful words, simple words. But somehow or another, they weren't getting very far with the problem of clean rooms. Parents wanted them. Kids didn't.

Rather than let this continue, I asked everyone to join me in a different approach. I asked if all of them would become teenagers for a little while. Everyone was to talk and think as a teenager. I went to the chalkboard and asked them to give me the reasons they had, as teenagers, for not cleaning their rooms. I wrote them down.

Honest things surfaced. "It's my way of getting back at my mom without hitting her." "I'm trying to show my independence." "I want my room to look like the rest of the house so my mom doesn't feel bad about how poorly she keeps our home." "What do you mean dirty?" The chalkboard filled.

It soon became apparent that a dirty room wasn't just a dirty room. It was often a message, though not a very clear one. As a matter of fact, we finally determined it could be a combination of more than 30 messages. But that's not the end of my story.

I then asked everyone in the room to become parents. Once again I recorded their answers, this time the reasons for wanting a room clean. "I'm afraid my picky sister-in-law will see that room and fault me." "I worry about the health of my children." "I need to exert authority and have it honored." "My mom never let *me* get away with a dirty room." Again, more than 30 different answers surfaced, all these from the parental perspective.

When the exercise was completed, the participants realized that even a topic as apparently straightforward as cleaning rooms offers the potential for sending many different messages, and thus creates many different problems. Left unattended, a simple, reasonable, and actually easily resolvable difference could escalate into outright family war. Most of those in New Orleans testified to times when that's exactly what happened.

What ultimately surfaced that day was a need for a method of making sure that things don't get out of hand—a method of problem solving. That's when I presented a very old six-step approach to conflict resolution. This six-step process for resolving family differences is something you'll want in your family first-aid kit. Let's look at it, step by step.

Step one: define the problem

Many families get tied up in squabbles at home and never really know what the squabbles are about. Oh, yes, each individual gives his or her opinion. But all the others disagree. Who is right?

Step one in problem solving builds on a commitment to agree to agree. Turned into practical language, that means everyone commits themselves to work toward agreeing on what the problem is.

Suppose the apparent situation is this: older brother refuses to take younger brother along with him to the store after his mother tells him to do so. When all participants are asked to define the problem, they answer like this: (*a*)

The mother says the problem is that the older son is disobedient and willful; (*b*) the younger brother says the older brother hates him and wants to avoid him; (*c*) the older brother says he wants to meet a girl at the store and he doesn't think he can do it with his younger brother tagging along. Now, you tell me: What's the problem? Whose perception is correct? And how will it (they) be solved?

If the "problem" is not defined to everyone's satisfaction, no solution will ever develop. There will be anger and bitterness and continued family squabbling. But if the problem is defined in a way that takes into consideration each person's view, some solutions might develop. So, first of all, there must be a clear understanding of the problem, and who owns it.

Step two: develop possible solutions

Please note that the word *solutions* in our headline is in the plural. If you have more than one person in the problem, you need to develop more than one solution.

Thinking back to the problem in step one, maybe one solution is for the son to simply obey his mother. The mother would agree to that. Or perhaps it could work out that the older brother might take the younger brother along but leave him at a friend's. The older brother would like that. Maybe another solution is to take the brother along and try to meet the girl at another time. You know who would like that. Or maybe it's time to make clear that the younger brother can't tag around with his older brother *all* the time and suggest that he go to a movie instead. Can you suggest more solutions?

There are really many possible solutions to any defined problem. Some solutions are usually better than others, but you'll never know that until you have laid them all out and evaluated each. If you can only think of one solution to a problem (and it just happens to be yours), then I suspect that the real problem is that you want your way. That's another kind of problem all by itself.

Step three: review your solutions and choose one

Sometimes the solutions surface quickly and, from the pile of answers, one stands out as obviously best. That's great. When that happens, choosing is easier. However, sometimes developing possible solutions and selecting one is a slow process. Many difficulties can arise to complicate the process. For example, some answers, good as they are, clearly have no appeal for one or the other of the participants in the discussion. That's when communication becomes very important, and times get tough.

But nice things happen, too, even in the toughest of times. In discussing a problem, new insights can burst on the scene and help all to sense a totally different, more creative solution that might otherwise never have appeared. New perceptions, new appreciation of other's needs, new recognition of communication complexity, new solutions to old tensions, new levels of relationship can all swell up out of this step-by-step process. These become special gifts to you and yours. The key to it all is the important understanding that, having defined the problem and having developed possible solutions, you must select one. That final choice must be made.

Step four: implementing your selection

Well, you've decided what to do. Now what? *Do it*.

I'm astounded how many organizations (and families) never get around to doing what they decide to do. They just spend their time solving problems, offering answers, and adjourning meetings.

There must be follow-through. Step four is the point of effort. It calls for action. Choosing a solution is not the same as solving a problem. Whatever you've decided ought to be done needs doing. Doing what you have agreed is required—go to the class, plan the picnic, delegate the responsibility, give the keys, let her choose. Whatever you choose as the solution, do it.

But that's not the end of this process. One step, maybe two, still call to us.

Step five: evaluate your choice

Once your answer is implemented, check to see whether it's working. Not every answer answers. Some can actually make things worse. Others expose aspects of the problem that were previously not recognized and further complicate the problem-solving process. Still other solutions settle one piece of the problem but fail to resolve others. For those reasons, continued evaluation is crucial.

What's exciting about the continued evaluation process for parents is that you get a chance and a reason to keep on talking with your teenagers. You continue talking to them about something that's easy to talk about: your joint concern. Because you've already taken the first four steps together, you are approaching a problem almost as peers, almost as equals. You are looking for a solution *with them*. Just as importantly, you are teaching them a process of problem solving that will bless them throughout their lives.

One of the greatest benefits of the problem-solving process is that, should step five show you have made an inadequate choice, the stage is set for step six: changing your mind.

Step six: if your solution isn't working, start all over again

If something you have decided to do doesn't work, that doesn't mean you should quit. It might mean you didn't understand things correctly, or that circumstances have

changed, or that people have changed. What do you do?
You go back to step one.

Changing your mind about a solution and backtracking
are not signs of weakness or intellectual incompetence.
Changing and backtracking are required when you have
inadequate information or have made an understandably
incorrect judgment. Real people don't always get things
right the first time, every time. That's why we need a process
for starting anew, for going back to the beginning.

If you don't admit failure, your family conversation will
be shot through with all kinds of subjects you dare not talk
about anymore. Doors will be closed on opportunities. But
if you work through this process to the end, including the
evaluation and backtracking if necessary, then the stage is
set for a successful approach to any problem that life can
bring.

Understand this: only the strong can change. It takes a
mature mom and an emotionally healthy dad to recognize
it's time for reversal and redirection. Weak parents are never
wrong. Weak parents stifle discussions and run over solutions with an abrupt, ". . . because I said so, that's why."
Their only way out of a difficulty is by ignoring or denying.
But the ignoring adds up and the denying makes things
worse.

Does this method really work? It sure does. I've used it
hundreds of times. There's really nothing new about it. I
don't even remember who first taught it to me. I have since
heard it described by a number of different names. I rather
suspect it was developed somewhere back in the earliest days
of civilized history. It's just a six-step commonsense approach to problem solving.

So there you have it: something else to include in your
family first-aid kit. Now you have two components: improved communication and six-step problem solving. One
basic ingredient yet remains: modeling.

The importance of modeling

How do we teach? I believe there are two ways. One is by words; the other is by example.

Which is best? I suspect neither is best. The finest teaching includes both. The finest teaching happens when word and deed are married. The finest teaching includes precept and example.

Precept (or "word") is a term used to describe organized and systematic teaching. Precept usually has to do with teaching principles. Your state's driving laws are precepts. The Ten Commandments are precepts. Family or school rules of conduct are precepts. Safety regulations are precepts.

We all need precepts to guide us through life. Whatever the precepts are called—laws, wisdom, philosophy, rules, recipes, commandments—we need them. Sons and daughters must know about precepts in life. Ignorance of precepts will not prevent problems. The damage will still be done even to youngsters who don't know it can happen.

Your children have a right to expect you to teach them appropriate precepts. That's one of the reasons God made parents. Teaching precepts is something parents can do. It is one of the main reasons for homes and families. There, in the home, among the family members, a great schooling should be taking place.

What precepts should be taught by parents? If I were to make a list, I would include religious beliefs; understandings about sex, marriage, and money; the value and method for development of life's goals; an understanding of the importance of family; the significance of keeping yourself physically well. All those need proper and regular presentation in the family. By the time your youngsters hit the teens, they should have been taught those and many other significant precepts, ranging from how to handle a sharp knife to what you say when you receive a gift.

But that's only half of the teaching task. If I had to make a choice between the two, I don't think it's the most effective half. Every presentation on precept must be accompanied by demonstrated example. Example is the much more emphatic teacher. What we see is more impressive than what we hear. Pictures beat words.

Years ago I was asked to champion the cause of family devotions. I traveled all over the United States doing so. In my presentation, I always talked about words and deeds. As an illustration of the weakness of words alone, I would ask a group to recall a dozen sentences that their parents had spoken to them during their years of being reared. Just a dozen.

You'd think that out of the millions of sentences a mother or father speaks to a child from birth to 16, a dozen sentences would easily surface. But try it yourself. See if you, right now, can recall a dozen genuine sentences from your parents.

Didn't do so well, did you? And if you remembered your dozen, what is that compared to all the millions that you've forgotten?

I made my speech one evening at a church in a little South Dakota town. Early the next morning an older farmer picked me up to drive me to the next town. As I entered his car a little after dawn, he said accusingly, "You kept me up all night!"

That fine man then rehashed with me what I had said about not being able to remember what our parents said, adding, "You're right. I can't remember a thing. But all night long I saw pictures. I recalled hundreds of things my parents *did*. It was like seeing a movie of my childhood, only it was a silent movie. I couldn't remember a single sentence with any degree of certainty."

That's the way it is. We don't remember words; we remember actions. We recall examples. That whole world of actions and examples is called *modeling*. Modeling is presenting to another person an approach to a problem through what we do. *That* we remember. We store up moments of the past, each one wrapped around someone's actions.

One of the bitter by-products of divorce is that many children grow up in a home without the daily positive modeling of both parents. Later in life, when they need to make a decision and turn to a parental pattern for guidance, it's as if that "reel" is missing from their memory's movie. That's tough.

Tone down the lectures. Instead, consciously be a model for your children. Once you have verbalized a precept, demonstrate it in you life—before their eyes. Do it in the way that you hope they will do it and continue doing it the rest of their lives. You can teach by your conduct. You *do* teach that way. I suspect it's the most effective way teaching happens. It's certainly the most remembered way.

An odd insight

Of the three ingredients for the family first-aid kit that I have listed, I believe the last—modeling—is most important. It's strange, but that's the one about which I write the least. The reason? There's not much skill development in modeling.

Modeling is showing yourself. Modeling is you. There are no specific classes in being a you. The only thing you can "do" is intentionally generate a more positive image. Maybe you'll have to change. Maybe you'll have to adjust things in your life. Those are important reasons for reading all kinds of books. Books like this give you a suggested standard. They encourage a change in conduct. They even teach you how.

There's another aspect to modeling that's important: you *do* model. It's not as if you will decide whether to model or not; you *do* model. Sad to say, many youngsters learn how they *don't want to live* their later lives by carefully watching their parents. That's negative modeling. It hurts families. It hurts people.

Our Lord Jesus Christ is the greatest example of effective and consistent teaching through precept and example, word and deed, that we have. He not only spoke about forgiveness, he lived it. He not only encouraged love, he was love. He inextricably tied word and deed together. One of the great Christmas hymns puts it clearly: "Love came down at Christmas." Love was the precept and love the action.

Why don't you read the four Gospels—all four of them? It won't take very long. Read the Gospels as if they were a textbook for teaching by precept and example. Look carefully at how Jesus verbally presented truths and then modeled those truths in his life. Jesus was a man of words and of deeds. In him you will find the best way to live with, and before, your children.

Most important for me is Jesus' living demonstration of earned and offered forgiveness. On the cross he earned and offered the hope that all failed parents, inadequate moms and frustrated fathers, yearn for. Through Christ, God forgives all of us for our pasts, and he urges us to try again, with Jesus' support. Via the promised coming of the Spirit, we can be led into truth. This truth not only has to do with our salvation and how it's earned and offered in Christ, but this truth teaches us how to live in the in-between time.

Concentrate on the three mini-subjects of this chapter. Collect each for the family first-aid kit. In so doing you will not only benefit your family, but you will develop more confidence in yourself. You'll find use for these same three skills in every other aspect of your lives. But then, I'm getting ahead of myself. Every other aspect of our lives is what the next chapter is all about.

7 Someone Wonderful— Like You?

At the end of our first book, Dr. Bardill and I inserted a page that allowed for and encouraged reader response. We got it.

As the responses began to flow in, I was at first mildly interested, then moderately amused, and finally fully amazed by our readers' most recurrent choice for "most interesting chapter." I thought the chapter on family, or the one on communication, or the one about getting along with friends would come in first. A few agreed with me. But far and away, the choice for most interesting chapter was one entitled "Learning to Trust Yourself."

Dr. Eric Ericson, a leading psychologist, would have anticipated the returns. It is his contention that developing self-trust is a primary task in life, that little maturing will take place without the development of self-trust. The little child who insists on tying his or her own shoe (though clumsily), or climbing the ladder of the slide alone (while frightening a parent to death), or even going to a friend's house "by myself" is actually intent on growing up through learning self-trust.

During the teens, that continuing task of learning to trust oneself is paramount. The specifics of the task will vary from person to person, but the overall experience is the same. Teenage boys, for instance, need to learn how to talk with girls. Girls will have to discover how to make friends of their mothers. Those two exciting adventures, and thousands of others just as important, are all part of the self-trust building that will take place if children are to successfully move into full-blown adulthood. But it doesn't stop there.

Trusting yourself—and learning how to develop more of that same trust—continues as a concern of first priority for the rest of life. It's true for parents too.

There are certain to be parents who are nervous about the title of this book. Because they don't know very much about teenagers or about what may be properly expected of them in their parental role, they're not quite sure they should thank God about teenagers at all! They are careful about their expressions of pleasures in rearing a son or daughter. But why?

It could be that their son or daughter doesn't give them many reasons for parental confidence and joy. That's possible. But the more likely reason for parental carefulness is their personal concept of the ideal parent. To put it simply, the problem with being a relaxed real parent is the imagined ideal parent.

Imagined ideal parents are the ones on TV whose house is always tidy and who, in any 30-minute sitcom, invariably figures out the perfect answer to their teenager's incredibly complicated need. And they do that every week! Year in and year out!

Ideal parents don't exist. There are no ideal parents. There never were. The image of an ideal parent only takes center stage when you decide to judge yourself—by a standard of perfection. However, when you judge yourself by what others are actually like, and by where you are on life's journey, the conclusions are very different. So get it straight—there are no ideal parents. There are only wonderful human parents like you!

Just as important as recognizing the tension between the real and the ideal is this comforting and true sentence: you've never been a parent of a single (or a second, or a third, or a fourth, etc.) teenager before. You haven't. Wherever you are in raising teenagers, this is the first time you've ever been there. You started out with no more knowledge about your teenager's coming adventure (and yours) than they did. You search, experience, and grow together. You'll make mistakes together too. Of greatest significance is this: in the process, you will both change and usually improve.

I still remember when our oldest daughter notified my wife and me, in a moderately accusatory fashion, that we weren't treating our younger daughter the same way we had treated her. Our answer was simple and direct: "You are right. We aren't. We got smarter!"

While it is true we did get smarter, the difference of treatment was more than that. We also got older. We became more experienced. Our financial condition improved. Our understanding of life deepened.

We tried to make clear to our firstborn that our treatment of her younger sister, while it was different, was no better than what she received. Younger parents bring to a relationship things that older parents do not. But the same is true of older parents too. Neither is better; there are advantages and disadvantages for both. We must simply recognize the difference.

There is one other factor too. No two children are exactly alike. (Ours surely weren't!) They become young adults in different styles. They have different needs. They bring different questions to us for which we, at different points in our lives, provide different answers. Each child is a blessing, but each in his or her own unique way.

That last paragraph is another way of saying that teens do as much for and to us as we do for and to them. They have the task of helping us become great parents *at the same time* that we are helping them become great sons and daughters. They know no more about their task than we know about ours. If we're both guided and informed by the other, the traveling is easier.

In addition, parents are going through *three* stages simultaneously. We are moving along as *parents,* as a *couple,* and as *individuals.* (I wonder who has the tougher task, parents or teens?) There's no way of avoiding those three simultaneous stages, mom and dad. They are there. Once my wife and I saw our tasks as being multifaceted, and that a lot was going on without our control or direction, we relaxed and tried to enjoy what was happening. We could start going about the business of rearing a family God's way.

God's way

God's way is not some kind of universal answer to every situation. *God's way* is a style, with some great specifics, of parenting teenagers. As we have seen (in Chapter 5), the cutting of the umbilical cord in the human birthing process is a perfect example of *God's way.* Newborns are immediately somewhat on their own, but they're never separated or alone. *God's way* includes surrounding those little tykes with people like you—parents, family, community, home. But God gives no one total control. No one can force a child, or even try to do so, without doing severe damage. *God's way* doesn't coerce. It operates with another power: influence.

Let me be more specific about the parenting aspects of *God's way.* *God's way* for parents includes three significant phases: (1) learning to trust yourself, (2) turning to God for forgiveness, and (3) helping your partner through those first two phases.

1. Learning to trust yourself

The road to self-trust begins with knowing as much as you can about the real person that you are, with relatively little concern about the ideal person you will never be. Discover the *real you* by reviewing the questions asked in Chapter 2, questions about all facets of your life: physical, spiritual, emotional, and social. Judge yourself, but remember: no judging based on perfection. Weigh yourself by genuine human standards.

If those questions are a bit difficult to work through, if they stir feelings of self-doubt, be of good cheer. That's the way they affect everybody. Only the vain, the hypocritical, and liars swarm through those paragraphs nodding in vigorous agreement at every place they think they ought. They are on top of all things physical, spiritual, emotional, and social. The rest of us get quieter, slouch deeper into our seats, and suffer a frustrated inner feeling that we have been so easily found out. And we have been. But the interesting question is, "Who found us out?" The answer? We did. You. Me. We found our own selves out!

That brings us to the Greek philosopher's goal (which is also biblical): *"Know yourself."* In the moments of self-examination, we are actually growing and, out of it all, developing a sense of self-trust.

Measuring yourself will require measuring others as well. They are our benchmarks. That means we must be every bit as critical and open-eyed about them as we are about ourselves. We don't do this in order to excuse ourselves, but in order to develop a reasonable standard for personal evaluation and for personal reinforcement at the human level. Without a basis for judgment, we'll never really know how we're doing or where we're going or how fast we're moving. Knowing yourself also means knowing others too.

Don't think studying yourself is going to be a continuous grim experience. I believe that most people discover they are much more dependable and reliable and competent and capable than they might have otherwise imagined. Searching ends up giving you a sense of self-confidence. Some of my best counseling happens when people come in with problems so complex that I get lost in the middle of them and then, after they have outlined the issues, I ask innocently, "What do you think you should do about that?" At first they are puzzled. They think I'm supposed to provide the answers. When it's clear that I'm not going to, they start unwinding their personal perceptions of what's possible. What great answers they give! Most of the time I listen to their solutions and finally say, "Sounds good to me. Why don't you do that?" My important role is authenticating their excellent personal solutions. They solve the problems, and realizing that they have solved them helps them trust themselves more.

Let me state it another way. People who look for help are usually much more competent at handling their problems than they think. Their searchings and questionings are actually healthy signs. They show a mature willingness to confront what might be an uncomfortable final answer. If that describes you, great. Keep on questioning.

By the way, next time *The Wizard of Oz* comes on TV, why don't you watch it. In your journey toward increased self-trust, you are like those travelers through Oz who discover at the hands of a wizard that there is much more going on inside themselves than they actually thought. You'll love that yellow brick road.

When I talk to teenagers about trusting themselves, I assure them it will result in four great things: *(a)* they will be more willing to take risks on future new adventures; *(b)* they will develop a more positive self-image; *(c)* they will stop being overwhelmingly jealous of others and others' accomplishments; and *(d)* they will realize they have capacities to improve, not only in areas where they know of their present special competencies, but also in areas that are new.

That four-point message to teenagers fits parents of teenagers too. When you determine to discover reasons to trust yourself, you have nothing to lose but your low self-image.

2. Turning to God for forgiveness

But what if your self-review shows there are many flaws and that you have a history of failures and an inclination toward errors? What if you, like me, must say, "I have failed"?

If? There is no if about it. Of course you have failed, and will fail again. All human beings fail. We fail because we are afflicted with the greatest of flaws: sin.

The four scriptural meanings of the word *sin* are: rebel, revolt, make a mistake, miss the mark. Two of those (rebel and revolt) signify active and intentional determination to oppose God's will. The other two, though just as consequential, are most passive and accidental in nature. The final result of all four is the same—someone has been harmed or, at the very least, not helped. What do you do when you meet failure—sin—in yourself or others?

The word that best describes what needs to happen when we meet sin is the word *forgive*. That biblical word has multiple meanings too. Specifically, it means three things: cover over, send away, let go. It does not mean forget. Once things have been forgiven, they ought to be forgotten, but that doesn't always happen. Kids keep telling me that. They talk about their parents' long-g-g-g-g memories that never let old matters rest. Parents say they keep bringing up the past because they want to make sure their teenagers have really learned. But no one learns by being told over and over again that they once (or twice or 20 times) failed.

God puts it this way: "I will forgive their sins and will no longer remember their wrongs" (Heb. 8:12). God lets our confessed transgressions rest. If we can't do that, we must at least realize that we need to do that. We need to suppress those urgings to keep rehearsing the sinful past and the confessed errors of our children and ourselves. That sentence, applied to your children, is good advice. Applied to yourself, it is a necessity.

We learn from mistakes when we are forgiven and are then empowered by the Holy Spirit to do things new and differently. Christians know the Holy Spirit as the great force that affects change within us in the face of our forgiven mistakes. He promises to direct people (Ezek. 36:27) and does. He promises to bless us with truth that brings wisdom and insight (John 16:13) and does. He promises to bring before all humanity the saving name of Jesus Christ (John 14:26) that forgives, and teaches us how to forgive, ourselves. That's how God handles sin.

But what does that kind of forgiveness do? How does forgiveness help us with our self-image and with developing trust?

First of all, when God removes his judgment from those who fail, the ominous threat of eternal punishment and God's recurring wrath disappear. Just knowing God forgives makes us feel better immediately. Then we are able to concentrate on the problem we face: the judgment of humankind.

We can then look at the judgment of humankind from the Christian perspective. What if others criticize and condemn us? Christians say, "If God is for us, who can be against us?" (Rom. 8:31). There's a thought for you!

Finally, if God can forgive me in Christ Jesus, I certainly can forgive myself. When I forgive myself, I will trust myself to try again, knowing that there is a satisfactory answer to my mistakes, whether past, present, or future.

Forgive yourself. Get on with living and building trust in yourself and in other human beings. But do that as a forgiving human being.

3. Helping your partner through those first two phases

Knowing you have been forgiven will calm you. It will also improve the way you deal with yourself—and your son or daughter. If you have those two aspects of your relationship straight, what about the third? How are things going with your marriage partner? Your son or daughter's teenage years could be a great time for you to review your relationship with your wife or husband.

Now don't get nervous. The review I have in mind will do no damage. It may surface a lot of debris, but that's not bad. When you know what's out there, you can do something about it! Many marriages falter and finally fail because people forget to review. Reviewing is really nothing more than remembering. Paul Ricour puts remembering in focus when he says, "Hope is the same thing as remembering." As you remember, and remember clearly, you have a basis for hoping that significant change will happen. It has in the past. So set aside an hour or two for remembering your marriage years with your marriage partner.

One good way of remembering is by looking at old photos, or by reviewing the calendar of your relationship, year by year. Hold up and study the pleasant times—the dark times—and the growing times. Handle the events tenderly as you turn them over and over while studying each from its many sides. You'll discover how many great moments there were. You'll also have a chance to reflect on yesterday's apprehensions, the times you really didn't know what to do, the actual fears that clutched you until a parent's best friend appeared on the scene: *change*.

Change is our greatest (and our inevitable) friend. Change happens. Sometimes it takes place in you. Sometimes it takes place in your partner. Change will take place in the boy or girl whom you now see as a teenager. Sometimes the changes that took place in the past were "learning" moments, even painful experiences that didn't have to be. But those taught too.

Over the rough road of all those past experiences, you made it! Both of you. Only those who have walked down the same road and worked together as partners can say, "*We* made it." That remembering, and clutching to the hope in change, can be the foundation for many further parental efforts, for encouragement, and for the assurance that you can and will overcome. Talk with your marriage partner. Let your partner and closest friend respond to you.

But what if you and your spouse have messed up things so completely that yesterday's landscape is littered with nothing but mistakes? What then? That's all the more reason for reviewing and sharing with your mate and then, hand in hand, talking to Jesus Christ. He knows the right kind

of things to say and says them. Here are some of Jesus'
words: "I forgive you"; "Don't worry, it will work out";
"I'm not leaving you—not ever"; "I can teach you to love
again." Those are the sentences Jesus says to people in need.
His speech is a model of what you can say to one another.

But what if you and your marriage partner are not in the
same faith place? What if your marriage partner has no faith
at all? He or she can't give you the encouraging and forgiving words. Even so, you're not alone. There are others.
God has surrounded us with others to help in moments like
that. A pastor? A Christian friend? Prayer? All those will
help you and can give you power to share with your marriage partner. Don't give up. Press on in Christ.

The late spring and early summer years of a marriage are
great. During those years, your teenager walks with you. It
is a time of many possibilities. You can grow, change, learn,
teach, love, build. You can do that for yourself. You can do
that with your teenager. You can do that beside your marriage partner.

Even if your marriage is in deep trouble—even if it's barely breathing—there isn't much that can't be undone. I've
seen too many impossible people and totally wrecked marriages reclaimed to ever give up. While many marriages are
in severe difficulty during children's teenage years, it's not
the teenager that causes the problem. That "credit" belongs
to a husband and a wife who haven't properly nurtured their
relationship or resolved their concerns. Take care of your
marriage and the tensions that arise within it. Take care of
yourself. Do both *under God's direction*. In the process, you'll
learn what you can really do by his power. In learning, you'll
trust yourself more. One of the first things God teaches you,
when you trust him, is that you are trustworthy, and that
you (I mean *you*) are really someone wonderful.

8 Making It All Work Together

Public speakers and authors face many problems. Two are fundamental. The first is stopping too soon—before the application is properly made. The second is rambling on and on long after a perfectly good ending or two has come and gone. Right now let's concentrate on the first. Let's come down hard in this chapter on the application—the "so what?"

Would you agree that there is nothing significant to be said on any family-related subject that does not build on Christ and is not grounded in his Word? That's not to say that everything to be known in life is packed within the pages of Scripture. It doesn't mean that Christ is essentially an answer man, offering endless specific resolutions to every one of our world's conundrums. But I do believe that our Savior is the way, the truth, and the life (John 14:6). He leads us to genuine understanding (John 8:32). I am convinced that Scripture is a stunning light of incredible intensity that brightens the darkest and most depressing human experience (Ps. 119:105) and evaporates fears of things within or without (John 20:19ff).

Even with that conviction, we as Christians are still faced with the task of gathering up all that this and other good books teach and somehow implementing their full insight in our families. Unapplied understanding is useless; it's like paint still in the can.

Remember how we began? We started by talking about the nervous apprehension (sometimes raw fear) that many adults experience as they first face teenage sons and daughters and the prospect of the teenage years. In the following pages we exposed myths and surfaced facts both about teenagers and about adults. We tried to hear the voice of Scripture on adolescence. We developed family first-aid skills. We focused on self-trust. We can't stop now. Three things yet call to us. Let's deal with them one by one.

A boundarying faith

As a pastor I believe in premarital counseling. I believe it's the best way to avoid major postmarital problems.

At my first meeting with a young couple, I take them into our church, walk them down the center aisle almost to the altar, and have them stand on the spot where they will later in the year speak their marriage vows. I ask them to lift their eyes and look a little to the left where, against the back wall of our chancel, stands a gigantic cross.

For the next few moments we talk together about their marriage. Will it be a lifelong Christian union, or do they have something else in mind? In one sense, we are deciding whether I will perform their wedding service. It's not that I must have things my way, but I believe that God must have his way.

Once they determine to make Christ a partner in their life together, it doesn't take long before we are talking about the heart of marriage. By the heart of marriage, I mean faith—boundarying faith.

There are two faiths. One is faith *that*. Faith *that* is factual faith. It deals with provable realities. Faith *that* is like knowledge. Examples of faith *that* would be our convictions *that* the earth is round, *that* ice is cold, *that* some monkeys live in trees, *that* sunrise marks the coming of morning.

As important as factual knowledge (faith *that*) may be, the more significant faith is faith *in*. Faith *in* is a faith that leans upon, that trusts, that dares. Faith *in* boldly claims forgiveness. Faith *in* knows that prayers are answered and fully trusts in the promises of God. Faith *in* claims all Christ offers in his redemptive act. It joyously accepts all Christ gives us by grace. Faith *in* boundaries. It draws a line. Families that tell the world about their faith *in* set themselves apart. Their faith becomes a separating boundary.

A boundary? Yes, faith *in* determines all kinds of boundaries. It establishes you or your family's sense of right and wrong (a boundary); how decisions are made in your home (a boundary); what values are to be claimed (boundaries, again); the way you view people, including teenagers, parents, and other important folk. You can recognize in a second when you are with a boundaried Christian family. You also know immediately when you are not, or when you are with a loosely-boundaried family.

Loosely-boundaried families make loose decisions. They are hard to pin down. Right and wrong blur. When the character of faith is fluid, vague, and ill-defined, the family decisions take on the same quality. Things never really settle down. How can they? No one even knows what "settle down" means.

When faith is clearly witnessed and sharply delineated, living is easier, decisions are more direct, and much conflict disappears. Well-defined faith boundaries make for well-defined faith families. And well-defined faith families make for peace.

But remember, it's faith *in* Christ we're using to establish the boundary. That kind of faith frees. It shows people how to achieve their fullest potential. It encourages exciting individualism and acknowledges with joy that, while we are all different, we have been made one in Christ. It drives away fear. It shows us how to confess wrong without destroying ourselves and how to forgive others without being weak.

There are at least two potential problems with having and maintaining a boundarying faith, though. Problem one is: "What if my marriage partner is not my faith partner? How can we set faith boundaries in our marriage if we don't have a common faith?" Problem two flows out of problem one: "What shall I do if that is the case?"

St. Paul deals with these problems, very directly, in 1 Corinthians 7. His advice to Christians is that they stick with their non-Christian marriage partners. His reasoning includes the question, "How do you know God hasn't sent you to that marriage partner for his (or her) salvation?"

But the truth must also be told. When husband and wife do not share a faith (faith *in*), a family's boundary will vary, as will almost everything else the family does. And please remember that we are talking about a faith-in-Christ boundary, not a faith in my church or my training or my family. Faith boundaries are not a matter of whether you are Episcopalian or Presbyterian, German or Irish, Smith or Jones. It's a matter of whether Christ reigns.

When Christ reigns in you, you can be the Christian witness. As a child of God, show your partner what it means to belong to him. Of course, teach your faith to your children. Help them to understand what you do and why you do it. Quietly, but persistently, press for the place of Jesus in family affairs.

And don't complain. Bear your burden with the greatest joy you can muster. Lift your head. Be Christ's man or woman in all you say and do. Put into practice the forgiveness that you have claimed from Jesus and offer it to others in his name. Then your own individual boundaries, under the Spirit's blessing, may become *your boundaries as a couple*. You may bring your partner to Christ. I've seen it happen many times.

I've also seen great Christian men and women continue to their deaths married to a faithless husband or wife. I've seen them strong to the end, even though they were saddened at the thought of missed memories. They continuously prayed for the salvation of their mate's souls, and they handled themselves in a way that brought words of blessing, even from the lips of one who did not understand faith's call.

If you are reading these words through the eyes of faith, thank God for that gift. If you read these words not quite understanding what they mean and not quite believing the good they offer, let me urge you to ask God for help. Remember, it says, "Ask, and you will receive . . ." (Matt. 7:7). Ask. God gives. God gives faith. *Only* God gives faith.

Practiced prayer

One exciting aspect of boundaried faith is prayer. The family that prays together (out of convinced determination to do so) stays together. Prayer becomes a uniting aspect of the boundarying.

I wish I could tell you that I have always had a full and active prayer life. That is not true. Oh, yes, certain kinds of prayers were a daily part of my life. I engaged in the "bread and bed prayers"—I asked a mealtime blessing and normally would offer my nighttime thanksgiving, unless I fell asleep.

There were public prayers, too, especially the liturgical aspect of congregational worship. I was trained and abundantly exampled by my parents in those kinds of prayers during my growing years. I'm glad that was so. Even those smatterings of prayer piety blessed me. If nothing else, that kind of praying regularly reminded me of who belongs to whom.

But programmed praying isn't all I have in mind when I add up the possibilities in prayer. There are other, freer-formed prayerful conversations in a Christian's life, prayers I didn't know of in my growing years. I love and use the ancient Collects and the stately prayers of the church. I turn to them for instruction, for edification, for spiritual encouragement. But now that I have found the "other" world of prayer, I am drawn there more and more. I believe that world gives me increased strength.

This kind of prayer that is better for me is actually little more than talking with God while holding the hand of someone who is ill or in need. I try to put into words my needs and feelings and the needs and feelings of my prayer partner. I use a little framework—a pattern—a prayer mold: ACTS.

That acronym, ACTS, reminds me that prayer should be: A—adoration, C—contrition, T—thanksgiving, S—supplication. Thinking about ACTS encourages a much more satisfying and wide-ranging prayer life.

Little by little, as I worked out my feelings in prayer, based on faith in Christ and careful listening for the needs of my prayer partner, I found that I was becoming a better pastor. I listened. I heard more. I saw the needs. Prayer was actually changing things. At the very least, it changed me.

I was at first confused, and then amazed, by how often the thing that was holding up positive change was me. Praying helped me realize that most things can be solved, or at least successfully confronted, if I can get my "me" in hand; if I get out of the way.

But that's not the whole of it. Prayer is much more than getting a hold on "me." Prayer is a power in itself. I've prayed for things beyond the ability of any human being and seen those prayers answered too often to question prayer's power. I've seen deliverance, healing, and change. I've seen immediate and amazing help. All flowed from prayer. But why not? Jesus said, "Ask and receive" (John 16:24). James tells us, "You do not have because you do not ask" (James 4:2). I accept both statements as truth. Yet we're still not done with prayer.

Prayer helps me discipline myself and, in the process, evaluate my learnings. I've learned to ask myself whether I really want a child so obedient that I don't have to be concerned with what he or she does, or a wife so passive before my will that her every hope is identical with mine. When you're asking for things from someone who can respond, you learn to ask in a different way. You learn to pray, as Jesus wisely taught us, "Yet not what I want, but what you want" (Matt. 26:39).

Looking back over my life, I'm amazed how often what I prayed for was actually much less than what I finally received. God gave me more, much more, than what I asked for or sought. Now that I know this, my "want list" is smaller and smaller. Now my desire is to walk closer and closer to the petitions of the Lord's Prayer. I see how pure those petitions are. Take time to seriously reflect on the Lord's Prayer—you will find it worth your while.

Remember how we started this section? We talked about practiced prayer that flows out of boundaried faith. Now, in faith, I pray "Thy will be done." That's not just an escape clause. It is my earnest desire. That bending before the will of God is a fruit of faith. It is a yearning that God would mold my life to his will so that I might receive all the best that he has in store for me. Faith and prayer are inextricably intertwined. They grow together. Sad to say, they decline together too.

How will you handle prayer in your life? And what is the status of prayer in your family? As I've already said, those questions are directly related to the faith of your marital team. One reason I believe Christians can say "Thank God I have a teenager" is my confidence that both parents and child are under the promised power of God to change whatever needs changing and improve whatever needs improving. That power is invoked through prayer.

The way of worship

I am a husband. I am a father. I am a pastor. Being a pastor does not change my responsibilities as a husband and a father. But being a pastor has one sure effect on the other two—it makes husbanding and fathering easier. Why? Because I get a chance to see, within the church, some of the greatest examples of husbanding and fathering this world has ever developed. I see those examples in many of my fellow members and coworshipers of Christ.

Now don't get me wrong. Over the last 30 years, I've had some awesome disappointments in people. I could tell you horror stories about the way Christians act that might tempt you to abandon the faith. And what I might overlook, Scripture will surely point out. The Bible does not hold back the stories of betraying Judas, doubting Thomas, flighty Peter, wicked Saul, hypocritical Ananias and Sapphira. It tells it like it is. It tells the *whole* story. So I'm willing to express my well-founded disappointments in the church, but I do so in hope. My hope is that the honesty will give credence to another observation just as valid and much more important: the church is the greatest institution this world has ever seen.

Think of it! The church, made up of flawed sons and daughters, of sinful pastors and vacillating parishioners, of selfish spiritual leaders and insensitive teachers, has done more to bless humanity over the years than any other organization in the world's history. The church historically set the pattern for establishing hospitals, for founding colleges, for developing laws to protect the weak. I won't list everything. All these things must be accepted as amazing when you consider the human element in the Christian church: the pastors and the parishioners. Looking at them, I'm surprised there aren't more mistakes and errors.

The reason our churches still function, with all their problems, is that God called the church into being. That biblical word *church* most generally refers to a local congregation, not some amorphous national or international body. That biblical church is where the people of God actually gather to receive strength, give encouragement, worship with joy, and participate in cooperative endeavors. That's the way the church functions—as people acting together. Individual

Christians need and look for a public, functioning, spiritual family. They *always* look for that family. Scripture is very clear: God makes no private deals with anyone. He doesn't offer some an independent relationship with direct access to him, apart from the rest of the Christian family, while the rest have to link up to others. The specific language of Scripture is so clear and so compelling on this point that no one can genuinely misunderstand it. We are family—connected. We are a body—connected. We are a community—connected. We are one people—connected. As a matter of fact, all the great, descriptive, collective words that describe God's followers on earth are plurals—no singulars.

What's the point? The point is that many people hurt themselves by assuming something can be done that can't be done. They think they can be Christians *alone*. They amputate themselves from the body of Christ and are surprised they feel so lifeless! The church is a local association, of God's origination, intended for you and your family. Get into it. Seek out a group where you can give of the fullness of his blessings to you and where you can receive the same wonderful things from others. And there will be blessings!

One blessing you will receive is an immediate diminishing of depressing loneliness and self-conscious separateness. In addition, in a congregation, you will find others who are facing the burdens and blessings that you are as a parent. They will help you. The church is looking for people it can help. By the Holy Spirit, through the fellowship of faith, the church takes all kinds of problems, reconditions them, and then hands them back to whoever brought them in the form of support, encouragement, new insight, and love. Isn't that great?

Think carefully about associating with a local parish. You need it. You need all it has to offer. It needs you. It needs all you have to give. It will bless you. It will help you be a blessing to others. That two-directional flow of favor is what God had in mind when he established those communities of Christ that we call local congregations.

And there is something else in that local community that will be a blessing: the pastor.

Pastors have always fascinated me. I am a pastor. Many of my friends are pastors. Over the years I've supervised hundreds of pastors. I have always found them to be re-markable blessings. However, they are remarkable blessings *only for those who use them.* While pastors don't know all the answers, they do know where many answers are and to whom otherwise unresolved questions can be taken. Most pastors know about God's system for healing hurts and for developing help in the world.

Here and there are scoundrels in the ministry. I won't say there are no problem children, but there aren't many. More amazing than the few failures is the exciting discovery of what a great reservoir of love and understanding, of care and sympathy, of wit and wisdom, of honesty, help, and hope pastors can be. God has raised them up as special people in his church. He gives them gifts and gives them as gifts to his people. That's what Eph. 4:11-12 is saying. Recognize and treasure what God wants you to have. Pas-tors are for your own good.

Find a pastor. Seek out a church. Then, putting the two together, start worshiping. Establish a way of weekly cele-bration with your family. Go to church.

Go to church? How's that going to help?

There are many wonderful benefits of worshiping. For one, it is a remarkable opportunity for the whole family to share a common experience. Where else do you get together and do something together? Where else is there a common experience, within the range of everyone's needs, that is applicable to your family day-by-day living? A shared wor-ship experience has the potential for introducing into the family significant subjects that might not otherwise be dis-cussed. Worship is a chance for family sharing and growth.

Worship is also a great opportunity for a cleansing, as the family confesses and receives the forgiveness in Christ. It sets the stage for forgiving each other. As a matter of fact, forgiveness from Christ to you comes in direct proportion to the way forgiveness to others from you is given. Long before there were communal hot tubs for physical cleansing and closeness, there was worship—a spiritual "hot tub" that had the same possibilities. It drew people together, made them better in that moment, and warmed them with a unity of faith at the cross of Christ. That's exciting.

But what if a church isn't exciting? What if it's dull, dull, dull? What then?

Make an appointment with your pastor. Express your desire for something better in worship. Cue the pastor in on what you think that better might be. Encourage practices in your church that answer your needs, whether it be finer music, more prayers, greater lay participation, different kinds of sermons. Get involved in the process. Discuss with your shepherd how, together, you can help better things happen.

And if nothing happens? Don't take this step too quickly (*you* could be the problem—not someone else), but why not look somewhere else? God didn't give us just one congregation. He gave us many. There's no blessing in steady spiritual dissatisfaction. And there's also no blessing in separation from worship either.

But the greatest benefit of all is that the worship becomes your way of joining the Magi, and the women at the tomb, and many others who brought gifts to Christ. You can bring yourself, your family, your spirit of faith, your public witness. And do you know what the Lord does with every gift brought to him? He receives it, multiplies it, repackages it, and gives it back. That's the kind of Lord he is. Worship will teach you that.

The boundarying faith; an improved prayer life; helpful and regular worship. There you have it. There's no better way to build family oneness, while each of you grows individually, than those three things. There is no better entree to joyful family living, to a clearer perception of yourself, and to an increased sympathy with and helpfulness for your teenager than through an understanding of those three things.

And if you take this chapter seriously and decide to walk that way? What happens then?

You will change. Your attitude will improve. Your perception of possibilities will expand. Everything will be different. The suggestions of this whole book will begin to make sense as in no other way. And, under the blessing of God, you will be ready to say out loud, "Thank God I have a teenager."

Now it's time for you to decide whether you will give life to the words in this book. I hope you decide to take the leap. All you have to lose is everything that has caused you trouble your whole life long. All you have to gain is the excitement of knowing truth, finding freedom, and experiencing full life in the Lord.